Also available at all good book stores

9781785313875

9781785315992

9781785317187

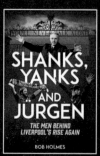

9781785316661

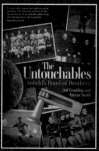

9781785318634

9781785319853

9781785313066

9781785311932

9781785314490

LIDDELL AT
ONE HUNDRED

LIDDELL AT
ONE HUNDRED

A Family Portrait
of a Liverpool Icon

PETER KENNY JONES

First published by Pitch Publishing, 2021

Pitch Publishing
A2 Yeoman Gate
Yeoman Way
Worthing
Sussex
BN13 3QZ
www.pitchpublishing.co.uk
info@pitchpublishing.co.uk

A CIP catalogue record is available for this book
from the British Library.

ISBN 978 1 78531 876 4

Typesetting and origination by Pitch Publishing
Printed and bound in Great Britain by TJ Books Ltd

Contents

Dedicated to the life of William Beveridge Liddell
Born – Townhill 1922. Died – Liverpool 2001.

A true sportsman and a great professional, Billy was
never booked or sent off in his entire footballing career.
A gentle and kind man with an immeasurable impact
on England's most successful football team, where he
spent his whole professional life. It has been a pleasure
getting to know you and I hope everyone who reads this
can further appreciate your ability, humility and status
within the game.

To live in the heart of those we love, is not to die.

Thomas Campbell

Acknowledgements

THE FIRST people I would like to acknowledge are all those I will undoubtedly forget to mention. I have been overwhelmed with the amount of help and support I have received from so many people; I really do apologise if I have not mentioned you.

The first dedication I would like to make would be to my Auntie Pat Taylor. Her battle with dementia and her death following COVID was a big blow to the family in the midst of writing this book. She was a massive Red and I know she would have loved to have been able to read this, as her battle with dementia also drew parallels to Billy Liddell's story. It is such a cruel disease.

My mum has had to deal with bad hand after bad hand since 2013. Losing two of her sisters and three battles with cancer has rocked my family hugely. My mum is a hero and the strongest person I will ever know. I want to make you as proud as possible and achieve as much as I can while you are here to enjoy the rewards with me.

The main man, my dad, is the reason I am football obsessed and he really deserves to have his name alongside mine on the front page. Ideas, research, transcribing, family trees, reading and checking – he has been a huge part of everything to do with this book and my life. I cannot thank you enough. Hope the black pudding helped though!

Rena Liddell, so much of this book was possible because of your generosity, heart and time. Hours on the phone during the lockdowns and letting me borrow family heirlooms and documents. Thank you for trusting me with this story and I hope I have done you and the Liddell name proud.

Jackie White, someone else who this book really could not have happened without. Thanks for deciding to do Scottish dancing and befriending one of the most famous families Liverpool has ever welcomed!

Annie, I have been a nightmare typing away in the garage while you had to sit with me and put up with the long hours I have had to dedicate to the book. Moving into our first house during the writing meant that we had to get my room ready as quickly as possible. Thanks for allowing me to pursue something I want to do for the rest of my life. I hope it is a success for both of us.

Thomas and Rebecca, my second parents. Supportive, helpful and always with my best interest at heart. If I had either of your brains, this would have been a lot easier!

Gray, I hope when you are old enough, you can read this and we can have a pint and a chat about Billy Liddell before a massive European night at Anfield together.

I do also need to thank Pitch Publishing for facilitating a dream and allowing me to write a book for them. I hope it sells well and that the next one is not too far on the horizon. Jeff Goulding, you were an early inspiration for me in my writing. I have always really appreciated how you would take the time to help with any stupid questions I had, and you made this small idea into something I thought could actually be achieved. David Cottrell, you acted as a mentor for me and I really appreciate you putting the belief in me that I could write a book. Stephen Done, thanks for all the help you have provided here and on several projects now. Tapas Iyer, the first man to believe in me enough to pay me for my writing, thank you. Murdoch Kennedy, I hope the George Allan mention is good for you!

All the interviewees, I have you all mentioned as much as I can because I wanted this book to be your words, not mine. The full list is in the testimonials and bibliography but thank you all so much for giving me your time and your memories. I tracked some of you down in some very unorthodox ways and I hope I did not come across as strange, as you may have at first worried I was!

Family members of the people I tried to track down, Bunny and Terry Melia, and Wendy South. Thanks for trusting me and for helping me. Alan Adamthwaite, Greg

Symon and Stephen Shaw for all your time and help too. Doug Cowie Jr, the time you took to help me was amazing; thank you so much.

Gudmundur Magnusson, Arnie Baldursson, and all the team at LFC History, your website is remarkable. The work you all put in is truly amazing and all football fans need to visit and appreciate your site. I have tried to give back in any small way possible by sharing interesting things I have found, but it is a drop in the ocean compared to how much you have helped me. Sites such as Play Up, Liverpool and the Facebook group Liverpool FC Historical Group are further examples of the fantastic community of Liverpool FC history that is out there. People so passionate about the club that they want to share their work and findings to help others, thank you all.

Rob Storry for allowing me to hold the 'Liddellpool' flag at Anfield, a moment I will never forget. Kieran Smith for your research into wartime football and your help with Billy's RAF career. Michael Makison for allowing me to use the fantastic squad picture. Adrian Killen for the use of your scrapbooks (and brain!). Jonny Stokkeland for your encyclopaedic help. Mal Winkles from Football Nostalgia on Twitter, the programmes were a big help. Chet Muraji, another expert in LFC's illustrious history. Jarek Zajac, thanks for all your help in tracking down some of the players on my list.

Dr Alex Jackson and Peter Holme at the National Football Museum Archives in Preston, thanks for all your help in my research and for allowing me access to some of Billy's Scotland shirts. Dr Jenny Gray from the RAF Pathfinders Archive and Rebekah Sharrock at the RAF Benevolent Fund, for your help with Billy's wartime activities. Susan Snell from the Museum of Freemasonry. The English and Scottish FAs, Liverpool, Chelsea and Portsmouth football clubs for allowing me to reproduce the programmes for the pre-order deals for the book.

Thank you to Dave Kirby who revised and rewrote his 2001 poem about Billy. I know this was written for your dad and I hope this book can be a tribute half as good as yours to Liverpool's generational hero.

Thank you to Paul Dicken and Liverpool Football Club, Neil Ward and Portsmouth Football Club, Amy from Chelsea Football Club, Simon Wickham from the Football Association, and Steven from the Scottish Football Association, for allowing me to reproduce and use some of the most meaningful programmes from Billy's illustrious career.

Warren McCann, thanks for our day trip at Anfield where you tried to make me look good. You are a true friend, thank you. Levon Bratt and Hannah Gibson, you gave me so much help at the early stages of the book with all your advice and answering of my stupid questions. Ollie O'Cal, the design guru, who helped make this front cover look so good! All my mates (Tom, Jon, Ryan, Chris, Sam, Jay, Hindle, Jack, Dan) and Seed City, who I had to let down several times in order to get this all completed; thanks for your support.

Everyone above and not mentioned, thank you all so much. This was hard work and the list of people I could remember to thank shows that it would not be possible without you all.

About the Author

THIS WHOLE process has been a pleasure and I am delighted to be able to present my first book. Born in Crosby, Liverpool in 1994, I have been a passionate Liverpool supporter since birth. My first match was against Roma at Anfield, in the same year as Billy Liddell unfortunately died, 2001. I was mascot for the club in an FA Cup fourth-round replay loss to Crystal Palace in 2003. The last home match I missed at Anfield, apart from behind-closed-doors matches, was in March 2011 and I have been lucky enough to watch Liverpool across Europe, Champions League Finals in Kiev and Madrid being the obvious highlights.

My football writing began during my studies at Liverpool Hope University, with my BA dissertation 'What were the social and cultural roles of football in Liverpool in the interwar period?' and my MA dissertation 'A Golden Age? A comparative analysis of Liverpool FC under Bill Shankly and Everton FC under Harry Catterick in the long decade 1959–1974'.

From my dissertations, I was able to write shorter pieces for several Liverpool and Everton fan sites. I tried to then write new articles about the Merseyside teams before broadening my writing on other clubs and countries. I then tried to make an effort to get my work printed in fanzines, which led to a push to get into official matchday programmes for English Football League clubs.

I was then approached by *Footy Analyst* for some paid opportunities, which was soon followed by a dream opportunity to write in the official Liverpool matchday programme and monthly magazine. From here I have been able to be a paid writer and have been trying to build my portfolio with writing and media appearances. Work for Times Radio, LBC and other football clubs has helped further establish me as a football historian and writer, closing in on 200 published articles and media appearances.

Following some thinking of my dad, he suggested some book ideas. I then pitched these to some publishing contacts I had acquired through a postponed ghostwriting opportunity. The sister of Billy Liddell, Rena Liddell, is good friends with my Auntie (Dad's sister) Jackie White, through their Scottish dancing connections. Without my dad, Jackie and Rena this book would certainly have never happened.

Fortunately, Pitch Publishing liked my ideas and writing and now I have written a book. I am really happy that people are willing to read my work and I hope you enjoy taking the time to go through it. I would love for this to lead to a full-time career in football in some capacity.

If you would like to read any of my other published work, it is all available on my website: https://peterkj.wixsite.com/football-historian or my Twitter @PeterKennyJones

I hope you enjoy the book and that there will be many more from me on a bookshelf in your house in the future!

Pete

peter.k.j@hotmail.com

@PeterKennyJones

https://peterkj.wixsite.com/football-historian

Preface

BILLY LIDDELL is without a doubt one of the greatest players to play for Liverpool. However, that alone does not justify writing a book about him 100 years after his birth.

Humility, loyalty, perseverance, power, kindness and the hundreds of other superlatives used in this book will best describe the man. Football is the most important of the least important things in life, a phrase coined by many of the greatest football philosophers in history, but William Beveridge Liddell personifies this.

It is impossible to ignore the social and cultural differences of Scotland in the 1930s and Liverpool in the 1940s, 50s and 60s, to football today. Billy did not have the financial benefits or distractions of the great players nowadays. His decision to join Liverpool was as much about job security as it was football. His mathematical talents, partnered with footballing ability, meant he had a happy and wealthy life in comparison to his peers, but nowhere near what it would have been had he been born 100 years later.

This book will delve into his life in a way that has not been seen before, not by solely studying facts, stats and match reports but by speaking with people and sharing their memories. The opportunity to speak with and share the memories of the calibre of people that have given up their time has been amazing personally but is really testament to the significance of the great Billy Liddell.

His life and era of football is on the brink of extinction and I really hope that this book helps provide the recognition he deserves. Liverpool Football Club does not begin with Bill Shankly. Had it not been for Billy Liddell, the 'dump' that Shankly labelled Anfield would have been in a much worse state and in a lower division.

The Second Division player plying his trade in England was repeatedly selected for Scotland and Great Britain. He had the team colloquially coined in his honour – Liddellpool was the name used and rightly so. He carried his club and the supporters and was able to hand them on a silver platter to the great Bill Shankly to take them on and achieve the greatness that he did.

Much is made of Steven Gerrard's loyalty to Liverpool. He certainly could have won ten times the number of medals he did at Liverpool had he followed the money and the silverware, but he remained loyal to his boyhood club. Billy Liddell left his home, had to wait nearly a decade for his debut and only won one trophy in his career, which was largely spent in the Second Division. If Gerrard receives praise for his loyalty, which he undoubtedly deserves, then Liddell deserves a fortnight-long fanfare for his undeterred devotion to Liverpool Football Club.

Many young Liverpool, Scotland and football supporters may either have never heard of Billy Liddell or be only slightly aware of his significance. I hope through reading this book that his story can reach a new and wider audience but also reignite the Liddell light for many older supporters. Speaking with those who loved him from near and far has been wonderful, and I hope their words and mine can elongate and eternalise Billy Liddell's deserved legacy.

Forewords

Jamie Carragher
Liverpool FC (1987–2013)

LIVERPOOL WERE called Liddellpool when Billy played. He was the Steven Gerrard figure of that era. This was a time when Liverpool weren't seen as the most dominant or successful team, but they had this player to hang on to and he was a player revered around the country, especially at Liverpool Football Club.

Billy was very unfortunate not to have the array of medals and European Cups that other players won in the future, because his team was not as good as those that followed. Anyone who was around the city in his era and looked back on Liverpool at that time would have known that he was one of the greatest figures in the club's history.

I always remember Ronnie Moran used to talk about the old players and he used to use it almost like a stick to beat the current players with. He would say we were never as good as the players that had gone before. It was a motivational tool and Liddell was one of the names that obviously popped up. He was amongst the list of great players of the 70s and 80s used to motivate us when we were playing in the 90s. No matter how well you had done or how well you were thinking you had done yourself, you were never of the level of those who had gone before you. Billy Liddell was always one of those names that was mentioned by Ronnie Moran.

Any fans today that are not aware of Billy just need to know that the Liverpool team was known as Liddellpool, and I think that just shows the impact he had. It's very difficult to get footage or to study too much of that era. There are probably only a very few players remembered from that time, it was such a long time ago, and Liverpool were not as successful before Bill Shankly came. We all know that he revolutionised the club, so those that came before Bill Shankly in some ways are forgotten. It almost feels like there's a line in the sand with Liverpool when Bill Shankly arrived in 1959, and we forget what went before.

You will see a lot of people pick their all-time Liverpool XI and Billy Liddell will find his way into a lot of the teams. I always think these types of players are hard to ignore. He could play left or right side, playing wide and getting goals, he is still prominent alongside the great players in the 60s, 70s and 80s. The fact that Billy Liddell is still in a lot of people's all-time XIs, considering what Liverpool have since gone on to achieve at home, abroad and since Bill Shankly came in, just shows how big a figure he was.

I believe any great football player would have been able to play in any era. I do not think you should ever dismiss and say anyone could not play now. The game is different, players are looked after a lot more fitness wise, but those players weren't born fitter, they are fitter because of a lot of advances in sports science. You are getting players that are better looked after and that is why the game is quicker.

Liddell is a Liverpool legend, there is no doubt about that. The difficulty he had in his career with the war, the people he played with and under, you just feel for him really. He was involved with two of the biggest legendary figures in Liverpool's history, who obviously thought a lot of him too. He played under Shankly, but if Shankly could have started maybe ten years before, the effect he could have had on Billy Liddell's career would have been huge. You admire these players more though. Yes, they have won fewer trophies and medals than others, but actually being there when it's not going so well shows loyalty when you are a top player. I think that is why Steven Gerrard is respected so much, not just in this country but around the world, because he stuck with his team through thick and thin. Liddell did the same and Liverpool Football Club was also his club.

With Liverpool there are so many legends of the club that you are not always going to get it right for everybody in terms of honouring their legacy. There are seven players that have benches named after them at Anfield, and the fact that Billy Liddell is in that group shows how highly he is still regarded by everyone at the club. I feel that is a huge honour for his friends and family that are still here now. That shows the club still remembers Billy Liddell. To only have seven out of the thousands that have played for the club, and managers that have managed the club, shows, I think, on its own how revered he still is.

I think it says it all that the banner is still there now too. Liverpool fans are great at remembering the former players and they never forget what they have done for them. I think he will always be remembered, but obviously as time goes by you will have younger fans that will probably know less about the past players. I'm certainly finding that myself! As time goes by, and certainly with the team doing as well as they are now, there are new heroes, but that is life in football. Any player that has still got a banner on the Kop 50–60 years after they stopped playing, I think they must have been some player and will never stop being remembered. That is some accolade in itself.

I think we're probably a lot more similar as people than as players. I'm sure he was very passionate about Liverpool and wanted things to go well. When they don't, you feel it personally but you don't look to move or change clubs. You look to put it right on the pitch and try to get the club back to where it was, or wants to be. In terms of players, we possibly could not be more different. One was a goalscoring winger, the other a tough-tackling defender and centre-back. I don't think there is much of a connection as players but everyone has to play in a team and everyone has to bring something a little different. I'm sure we could have worked it out in a team and it would have been a nice blend. Billy didn't drink or swear, but I'm sure opposites can attract!

Ian Callaghan
Liverpool FC (1957–1978)

I WAS 13 when I went with my mates in the Boys' Pen and the anticipation when Billy got the ball was just unbelievable. Liverpool was a Second Division club but the anticipation from the crowd when he got the ball was just immense. I became a Liverpool supporter because of Billy and then when the opportunity did arise for me to play for Liverpool or Everton, I chose Liverpool because of him. Although Everton were a First Division club and my dad was an Evertonian, I still chose Liverpool. It upset my dad, but it was the best thing I ever did. To then go on and have the opportunity to take over his position at outside-right, it was an honour.

He was a lovely, lovely man. He was quietly spoken but gave me so much advice. Billy wasn't just a professional footballer, he was an accountant, he was a Justice of the Peace, he was just a special man and he really was an unbelievable player.

He was a Scottish international and the Liverpool supporters would call the team Liddellpool, which shows you the impact he had on this football club, and he is one of the greatest to ever play for Liverpool, without a doubt. He was a quiet man, not what you would call a shouter, and he was coming to the end of his career when I was playing for the reserves, so I don't think there were many games we played together before he retired. Billy never went anywhere else and never played for another club. He was so loyal to Liverpool for so many years.

He was just a tremendous player. His attributes were that he had a phenomenal shot and he was a good header of the ball. He was just a great player. You must be great for the fans to call the team Liddellpool – he was outstanding. He was finishing when I was just coming in, but all the players that can remember him had an unbelievable respect for him because he was such a great man.

When I think back on my career, and I had a long career at Liverpool, taking over from the great man is up there with one of the best things I ever did. I really mean that, it was fantastic to take over and even to play with him in the reserves was a great honour.

Alan Hansen

Liverpool FC (1977–1991), Scotland national team (1979–1987)

THE FIRST time I ever met Billy Liddell, I knew him only by the reputation of being one of the best footballers of that time who had played for Liverpool, probably the best. What really surprised me was the demeanour. He was the friendliest and most approachable guy that I think has ever been at Liverpool. Between Billy Liddell and Ian Callaghan, I think there is a lesson to everyone that plays football on how to conduct themselves. Billy was beyond friendliness; he was just awesome. Always smiling, always ready to speak to you, always engaging and he was just brilliant, absolutely brilliant. I used to love talking to him whenever I met him in the Players' Lounge.

His wife Phyllis was a real character as well. He was quiet, but she was more outgoing and the two of them were a perfect partnership. There were certain people that everyone would gravitate towards in the Players' Lounge and Billy

Liddell was one of them. I was lucky enough that, over my years with the club, I met him on quite a regular basis. He used to go to all the games and you would always see him in the lounge. Sometimes I would go and look for him so I could spend five minutes talking to him, especially if I hadn't done so in a while. He was a part of Liverpool's heritage; he was a fixture of the club and everybody loved him. He was a true gentleman and he never got above himself; he was always on an even keel and just a delight to talk to.

He would always say to us that we were doing well. It didn't matter if you were terrible, Billy would say, 'You're doing well!' He was always the same, always affable, convivial and just great to talk to. The fact he has been immortalised with a bench by the new Main Stand is a testament to what he did while he was at Liverpool. Obviously, we're talking about a long, long time ago, but he has been remembered by the fans. He played in the 40s and 50s and for him to still be remembered is again a testament to what Billy was all about.

I was never lucky enough to play with him and there isn't enough footage to appreciate what he did. However, when you listen to the stories and you read the reports, it's clear that he was right up there with the best of them.

Testimonials

Betty Liddell – Sister-in-law

He was ever so quiet. He shook my hand and said, 'Pleased to meet you,' but a very quiet man. He was his own person, but he was lovely. He had a lovely family.

David Liddell – Son

He was very straightforward, he was fast, and of course he scored a lot of goals. I think that's why the Kop just took to him, as well as his work ethic and loyalty to the club.

Malcolm Liddell – Son

I would sum him up by saying he was a father figure; he was my father and he was a great footballer.

Rena Liddell – Sister

He played for Liverpool, received many an accolade, and was very happy in what he did. He wasn't a boaster and didn't go on about what he had done, he just enjoyed what he did. He enjoyed playing football and enjoyed life after football. Most of all he was my brother and family through and through.

Tom Ogilvie – Cousin
They called them 'Liddellpool' instead of Liverpool, but he always said there was everyone in the team, it was not just him. He was that type of man; he did not want all the praise.

Pat Martin – Parishioner of Court Hey Methodist Church
If Phyllis didn't want to get up and dance, he would get one of the other ladies up to dance, myself included, but I could never dance as good as he did.

Ian Tracey – Family Friend
A true 'gentleman' in every sense of the word, and lovely Christian man, whom it was my immense privilege to know, and moreover to be able to call 'friend'.

Alan Banks – Liverpool FC (1956–1961)
He is one of the best players that has ever played for the club. I put him alongside Kenny Dalglish and Steven Gerrard as the three best players ever to play for this club. When you consider all the best players we've had, counting the present-day players, that's how high I rate Bill.

Alex South – Liverpool FC (1954–1956)
A gentleman, a scholar, and a fine football player, he was some player was Billy. Once he got on a run with the ball, by Christ he took some stopping. He was like an express train down that wing! He was a household name and they adored him, and he couldn't do any wrong. He deserved to be praised because he was such a wonderful player.

Billy Howard – Liverpool FC (1956–1962)

Football has changed, and different stars have come along, but Billy was the original star for me. There may have been players going back into the 1800s and maybe bigger stars then, but Billy was Mr Liverpool. Apart from being a top player, Billy engineered spirit in the fans just by playing for us.

Doug Cowie – Scotland National Team (1953–1958)

He had the type of build that he looked strong and speedy. You thought just by looking at him that he had a good chance of pushing the ball past the full-back and beating him for speed and that was really his game; he was direct. Rather than looking for short passes inside, he was more likely to get up the line and whip the ball across for team-mates or cut inside for a shot at goal.

George Scott – Liverpool FC (1961–1965)

He had time for everyone, considering what he had achieved. He achieved everything in the game, played over 500 times for the club and scored over 200 goals. Shankly told us all at the beginning that the club was called Liddellpool. He carried that team, there were some good players, but Billy was the main man. I would say he was one of the top three players that Liverpool ever had.

Gordon Milne – Liverpool FC (1960–1967)

Billy was unassuming, he was helpful to young players, he was always talking to me in training and the short time that I worked with him. It's probably old-fashioned to say now, but he just came across as a proper gentleman and a wonderful ambassador for football, never mind what he did for the club.

Gordon Wallace – Liverpool FC (1961–1967)

I can understand why people used to tell us as kids about Billy Liddell and how powerful his shooting was. He could head the ball, he kicked with his left and right, he had everything. He was a remarkable man.

Ian Callaghan – Liverpool FC (1957–1978)

I went in the Boys' Pen when it was in the Kemlyn Road Stand and the enthusiasm from the crowd when Billy got the ball was very special. He really was a great player and a really lovely man as well.

Jimmy Melia – Liverpool FC (1953–1964)

He was amongst the best five players that have ever played for Liverpool. Two-footed player, terrific in the air, two great feet, right foot and left foot, and he was that good at Liverpool, they called them Liddellpool.

Johnny Morrissey – Liverpool FC (1955–1962)

Liverpool have had so many good players but most of the players Liverpool had when he played were fairly good or average, but not great. He was the first great Liverpool player in my eyes, definitely!

Keith Burkinshaw – Liverpool FC (1953–1957)

He was a player that other players looked up to, the most influential player at Liverpool while I was there with regard to the winning and losing of games, because he was the one who scored the most number of goals and he had a big effect on the team.

Alan Hansen – Liverpool FC (1977–1991)

He was the friendliest and most approachable guy that I think has ever been at Liverpool. Between Billy Liddell and Ian Callaghan, I think there is a lesson to everyone that plays football on how to conduct themselves. Billy was beyond friendliness; he was just awesome.

Jamie Carragher – Liverpool FC (1987–2013)

Liverpool fans are great at remembering the former players and they never forget what players have done for them. I think he'll always be remembered.

Norman Gard – Former Liverpool FC Player Liaison Officer

He is everything the modern footballer isn't. He was respected, he was like a pillar of the community. He was a great player, strong and dedicated and would still have made it today.

Paul Moran – Son of Ronnie Moran – Liverpool FC Player and Coach (1949–1998)

People asked my dad about Billy Liddell; he used to say that when he was starting up at Liverpool, while Billy Liddell was there, any good habits or anything he thought could help him, he picked them up from Billy. He said he was an absolute leader in the dressing room and my dad admired him.

Dominic Myers – Colleague at the Guild of Students at University of Liverpool

Gentle and not wanting to bring the attention to his glory. I did ask him if he had met Bill Shankly and what he was like (very naive of me). He gave me a wry smile and something along the lines of 'a very special man for Liverpool'. In those days I gave a lot but hadn't learned the skills of listening and pausing … such a wasted opportunity.

Adrian Killen – Supporter
From what I saw of him in his later days and what I've read about him, as well as what my grandparents, parents, brother and all the others supporters have said, he has to be possibly the best player that ever played for Liverpool Football Club.

Bill Hughes – Supporter
Billy was just a nice guy, who we all knew and loved. He was top of the tree, as far as I'm concerned, as a player and as a man. I was in awe of him.

Frank Cann – Supporter
My very first memory was seeing Billy in 1954, the first game of the season when we had come down to the Second Division and we played Doncaster Rovers. The first time I saw Billy, because he was talked about that much in our house, the hairs on the back of my neck stood on end. I've never had such a thrill since and I've seen six European Cups and 19 leagues, but the first moment I saw that man was etched in my mind forever.

Fred Wilson – Supporter
The greatest man ever in football that I've ever known, without a doubt, and I've seen some greats like Kenny Dalglish, Ian Rush and Graeme Souness, but nobody comes near Billy. I think he was the greatest thing to ever happen to Liverpool Football Club.

John Carey – Supporter

He played on the wings and at centre-forward, he could head a ball, he was two-footed, he could tackle, he could dribble. He was a good all-round footballer and you never heard him shouting or bawling, because he was a gentleman too.

Phil Cummings – Supporter

Billy was my first hero. One game he played on after a head injury, which meant he came back on to the pitch with an old-fashioned bandage around his forehead. Every time he got the ball that game, the Kop would chant, 'Geronimo!' He was the fastest forward in the game, the hardest shot on the run and the hardest header of anyone in the game. The fans used to wait for him to get the ball on the halfway line, and as he got nearer the goal, it got louder and louder. It was spine-tingling.

Tommy Jones – Supporter

I never knew my dad, he died when I was a baby. I only have stories told by my mum and my uncle. But Billy was undoubtedly my dad's hero. I've always felt closest to my dad on the Kop at Anfield. From the stories I've heard, Billy gave the red half of the city pride. He was obviously a great player and very strong on the ball, but his humility still shone through.

I loved those qualities in my hero Kenny Dalglish. Both were real team players. Billy was also incredibly loyal, like Steven Gerrard. Both had offers to leave but they stuck around when times were hard. For Billy to stay when they were in the Second Division speaks volumes about the man. Billy was my dad's hero, Kenny was mine, Stevie is my lad's. That spans eight decades of Liverpool Football Club. I have an emotional attachment to all three and Billy started it.

Paul McNulty – Supporter

He was well respected throughout the city. Everybody you spoke to would say he was a gentleman, he was a great player on the pitch and a great man off it. He was a true gentleman, which you don't get now.

Ron Schofield – Supporter

We had the greatest players that world football has ever seen. He was a Scottish international, he was an outstanding player, could use both feet and he could head the ball. He played the game in a sportsmanlike manner and was a gentleman on and off the field.

Townhill, Growing Up,
and the Liddell Family

BILLY LIDDELL'S story begins in a small Scottish village called Townhill, just north of Dunfermline, in Fife, Scotland. Food, or the lack of it, was a major part of his early days. The staple diet of mince and tatties was often on the menu and Billy was habitually mocked for being such a slow eater.

Although his life certainly later moved to Liverpool, he was very proud of the place where he was born. Townhill has become a village synonymous with Billy Liddell, honouring the man with the 'Billy Liddell Sports Complex'. There stands the cairn memorial with a plaque that has the following inscribed:

William Beveridge Liddell
The garden and memorial cairn are dedicated to
the memory of Townhill-born football legend
Billy Liddell.

Billy began his football career with Kingseat
Juveniles then Lochgelly Violet.
He spent his entire professional career with
Liverpool Football Club, signing in 1939 and
making 534 appearances scoring 228 goals.
His contribution to Liverpool was such that the
club was nicknamed 'Liddellpool'.
Billy was capped 29 times for Scotland and was
one of only two players to appear in the Great
Britain team of 1947 and 1955.
A true sportsman and a great professional,
Billy was never booked or sent off in his entire
footballing career.

Born – Townhill 1922. Died – Liverpool 2001.

Evidently and understandably, the town is very proud of him.
William Beveridge Liddell was born on 10 January
1922, the eldest child of six. He had four younger brothers:
Tom, Campbell, Alistair and George, the latter being the
twin brother of Billy's only sister, Rena. The twins were the
youngest siblings, being born 17 years after Billy and while
their mother, Montgomery, was 42.

| James Liddell | Montgomery Liddell (Wilson) |
| 05.11.1896 – 29.01.1951 | 06.10.1897 – 07.1969 |

William Beveridge Liddell	Thomas McLean Wilson Liddell	James Campbell Wilson Liddell	Alistair Andrew Liddell	George Izzat Liddell	Rena Liddell
10.01.1922 – 03.07.2001	13.09.1923 – 22.01.1966	1929 – 03.02.1989	21.05.1935 – 12.1996	12.09.1939 – 10.09.2004	12.09.1939 –

The strange forename of Montgomery came from the Scottish tradition of using surnames as middle and first names of children, to keep the mother's maiden name alive, Montgomery being in the family as far back as the 1700s. This strong sense of Scottish family tradition caused Montgomery countless embarrassing moments. 'Mr Liddell' would often be called in doctors' surgeries and places alike, before confusion as Mrs Liddell would have to explain her peculiar first name!

The real Mr Liddell was James, a miner continuing the family trade from his father William. Life for an early-20th-century miner in Scotland was far from easy. James worked in Muircockhall Colliery, mining coal amongst 200 other men in Townhill. Long hours, little-to-no health and safety consideration and equally low wages meant that the family home was a cottage with no inside toilet for the eight inhabitants.

No one within the family continued James's mining profession, as per the instructions of James, who knew the health dangers attached to the job. So, the Liddell parents were keen to ensure that all six children were supported by a trade as they entered working life. Aside from going on to dominate Merseyside football for a couple of decades, Billy's talents in the working world came from his mathematical ability. Having always been strong at maths all the way through school, he was set to pursue a career as an accountant to sustain his footballing passion, or to fall back on in case of injury or simply not being good enough to play at a high level.

Billy's siblings also did not follow their father into mining, nor did they possess the mathematical skills of their eldest brother. Tom was a footballer turned cobbler, Campbell a grocer for the Co-Op in Blairhall, playing football for his work team. Alistair was a baker and the least interested and talented footballer. He enjoyed rugby and swimming in his spare time and the family would all purchase tickets to attend his galas. The twins George and Rena both did office work, George playing five-a-side football with his friends. It is testament to their parents that they would all go on to have varied lives away from Townhill, but this was largely down to Billy's footballing talents that uprooted them from their family home in 1951.

Before Billy attended primary school, Montgomery would use his excitement, energy and already obvious athletic ability to run messages around Townhill. Despite his jet-black hair of his Liverpool heyday, the fair-haired Billy would deliver the messages with a small ball at his feet. He was constantly honing and improving his skills by rebounding the ball off kerbsides and working on his technique. The best evidence that his skills were being built rather than perfected was the fact that with every message that he delivered for his mother, he often asked the recipients, 'Whaur's ma ba?' (Where's my ball?)

As James was a coal miner, he worked long hours down the pits, so Billy was closest to Montgomery. The relationship remained strong after Billy left home, with the weekly letters the two would write to each other after church on a Sunday. When Montgomery ended up moving to Liverpool, the bond grew stronger still and they had a very close mother–son relationship.

Billy's love for football came from his father, grandfather and his school. Despite playing football locally, James Liddell was not the man that Billy's inherited football talents would be attributed to – it was James's father, Billy's grandfather, William. He played to a high amateur standard in Scotland as a centre-half and could see the obvious ability that his grandson possessed. Billy's father would also encourage his football and take him to watch Dunfermline with the rest of the Liddell boys.

In a way to encourage Billy, William would give Billy a penny for every goal he scored. This near enough bankrupted him during Billy's early days at Townhill Primary School, Kingseat Juveniles and Lochgelly Violet, so much so that he had to swiftly lower the price! Billy's goalscoring initially improved but soon started faltering. Whether it was a young Billy's negotiation tactic or just a dip in form, William then promised twopence for each goal. Miraculously, in the next match Billy's goal drought ended as he scored nine goals. He was mischievously happy to inform his grandfather of the money he was owed.

However, Billy's first-ever footballing appearance was as a six-year-old goalkeeper in a local five-a-side kids' tournament run by Townhill Industrial Co-Operative Society. Billy played in goal for the opening minutes of his first match but, as he conceded an early goal, he was released upfield and quickly ran riot.

By the age of seven, Billy was playing for Townhill Primary School, who he went on to captain, and played against boys three years older than himself. James Liddell was called into school one day as Mr Wilson, the headmaster, had been approached by neighbouring school headmasters who had requested proof that Billy was only seven. James quickly provided proof of Billy's age and ended the arguments.

Playing above his years no doubt hardened Billy's game from a young age, but this was to the detriment of the Scotland Schoolboys selectors. He did manage to make his way into the Scottish Schoolboys against Ireland and England in 1935 but, despite his obvious talents, he was so small that he was often overlooked because of his physique. Billy then played briefly for Townhill Keep Fit Class before joining Kingseat Juveniles when he was 12, getting paid 12½d a match.

Frustratingly for some of his peers, Billy was not only the footballing hero, but he was a real academic. He was the only one of his siblings to attend Dunfermline High School, whereas the rest went to Queen Anne, the difference between the two being that essentially Billy attended a grammar school for the more academically gifted children and the rest of the Liddells attended the comprehensive school. He was a bright student, doing well in his exams and excelling in maths. His good behaviour meant that he was not too often on the receiving end of 'the strap', the horrendous punishment tool at the school. Billy's attendance at Dunfermline High School also gave him access to better sporting opportunities in both rugby, which he disliked, and football.

His academic ability was first displayed through the bursary he was awarded for the high school, where he studied for his higher leaving certificate. He played for and captained the school's football team, and also played for the rugby team and the cricket team, for which he was a competent batsman. Being the all-round athlete he was, Billy also won eight medals for track and field events in the school, all while achieving high grades, attending the Townhill church choir and teaching in the Sunday school.

When he reached 15, the local junior clubs were keen to take Billy and it was Lochgelly Violet who managed to secure his services, paying him 7s. 6d. a match. He only spent one season with the club, but this was enough to attract a lot of admirers from further afield. Scouts from Partick Thistle, Hamilton, Manchester City and Arsenal were on the scene quickly and Liverpool were soon to follow.

An interesting aside to the origins of football and rugby in Britain can be mentioned here. Upon researching the footballing periods of Billy's prominence, it becomes quite glaring that football is referred to as 'soccer'. Indeed Billy's own autobiography is titled *My Soccer Story*. When the word soccer is used in reference to football in Britain today, it is scoffed at as Americanisation of 'our game'; however, the origins of football, soccer and rugby intertwine.

In a very simplified version of the tale, during an early Football Association meeting in 1863, the laws of football were outlined. This was at the time that the rules of rugby were also being drawn up. Rugby was then known as rugby football and football as association football. In a way to ensure that the two were not mixed up, rugby football was shortened to 'rugger', and association football to 'soccer'. Although this was used quite colloquially in the late 1800s, it became the more highbrow and old-school way of referring to football in the era of Billy Liddell, in the 1940s and 50s. Therefore, many newspapers and books used 'soccer', but the word has almost entirely died out from British terraces today and has now become a stick to beat American football fans with.

The Liddells' early football (or soccer!) encounters were between Cowdenbeath and Dunfermline Athletic. The Liddells supported Dunfermline and their cousins, the Ogilvies (Montgomery's sister's family) supported Cowdenbeath. Although the two teams are traditional rivals, the family connection meant that the boys would travel between each team on matchdays. One week they would don the black and white of Dunfermline alongside the Ogilvies, the next they would be with them in Cowdenbeath cheering on Cowden.

Billy's love for Dunfermline was diluted with his move to Liverpool; however, the boys in the family would still attend Dunfermline matches without Billy. Meanwhile, one of his cousins, Tom Ogilvie, went on to be a ball boy, scout, stadium announcer and secretary for Cowdenbeath. Tom's love for the Blue Brazil shows the importance of football to the wider family and the loyalty and sense of community that football brought them all.

Rena Liddell, the only female sibling of Billy, is also football mad. One of the earliest presents she received from the family was a pair of football boots so that she could play with her twin brother George. She is now a Liverpool season ticket holder and lives within a stone's throw of Anfield.

The 17-year age gap between Billy and the twins Rena and George meant that much of their early childhood was spent supporting their brother from afar. This being the days before television and the fact that they lived in Townhill meant that, as they could not get the train to Liverpool every week, their knowledge of their brother the football star was often through the radio for Scotland matches. As the family gathered round the wireless to support Billy, one thing would be of constant annoyance to his father, James.

Whenever Willie (or Wully), as Billy was often referred to in his early playing days, had the ball, they would refer to him as 'Willie Lid-ell' and James would shout at the radio, 'It's Liddell, you idiots!'

The surname did seem to cause a lot of problems in Billy's formative footballing years. One article that was just 19 lines long and discussed how Tranmere Rovers refused to take Billy on loan (a decision I am sure they lived to regret), only managed to spell his surname correctly once in three attempts! One article even described Billy as an up-and-coming Chinese winger called Li Dell!

Despite these inexplicable surname complications, Billy would intermittently return from his footballing exploits to see the family as a local football star but without an ego to match. This was a different time where fan adulation culminated in a 'hello Mr Liddell' and a polite request for an autograph; however, Billy never made any of his family feel as though they were living in his shadow. He would return from football or from the war to see his brothers and youngest twin siblings, and they would laugh and joke as he threw the twins around like a rugby ball. Despite the family becoming increasingly known as 'the brother/parent of Billy Liddell' to the Townhill and wider Scottish and British communities, Billy never let it go to his head and remained kind, softly spoken and level-headed.

Another important part of Billy's early life in Scotland was religion. The Liddells were a very pious family that would spend their Sundays in church, including at Sunday school. Billy was a staunch Christian and these values were the key reason why he never drank and never swore. He was a very morally righteous man and, without being outspoken, he was very proud of his religion.

Without a doubt, Billy's religious beliefs made him a better footballer. Not because God scored over 200 Liverpool goals for him, but because it gave him the drive and strength of will to play until he was 38. He was ahead of his time in that he had a great diet and was incredibly fit. Much is made of sports science in the modern game, and one can only imagine the extra years he could have added on to his career, beyond him being the oldest ever post-war outfield player for Liverpool when he retired.

One of the first to follow Billy out of Townhill was Tom, the brother that he was closest to. This was not just because of the one-year age gap between the two but they also shared a love and ability for playing football. Unfortunately for Tom, he was no Billy Liddell and, despite having the opportunity to sign for Liverpool in 1949, he never managed a first-team appearance.

After Tom's exit from Liverpool, his career never really took off, which led to him dropping out of the game. The Liddell family plan of a trade to fall back on meant that he would then go on to become a full-time cobbler. However, this decision nearly killed Tom prematurely as he was diagnosed with cancer. His cancer was of the oesophagus, which doctors attributed to him putting nails in his mouth during his work as he would hold them there before spitting them into his hand ready to hammer them.

Tom endured a terrible end to his life following his diagnosis of throat cancer in the late 1960s as he was unable to swallow. After many operations, first stretching the gullet and then inserting various prostheses, he was unable to eat solid food and he passed away in his fifties. Billy was crushed by Tom's death, losing a brother and a great friend.

Unfortunately for the middle Liddell brothers, disease and illness was a big part of all of their lives. Campbell was also diagnosed with cancer before he died of the disease in 1989 and Alistair died of a heart attack in 1996. Their mother, Montgomery, passed away in 1969 of a brain haemorrhage. Only Billy, Campbell and George had children but through Campbell the Liddell family lives on in Townhill as his family remains in the area.

Although Billy moved to Liverpool in 1938, this was not the reason that the family left their home. The death of his father, James, when he was 54, in 1951, turned the family upside down. As the eldest male in the family, Billy took the Liddell helm. He took charge of the family, moved them into his Liverpool home and found himself a new house so they could live in his – all this at the age of 29. But the story of Billy Liddell will always begin in Townhill and it is a small village that played a huge role in creating a hard-working, virtuous and football-mad family.

2

Moving to Liverpool

June 7th, 1938.

Dear Mr Liddell,

On Sat last I interviewed the Secretary, Treasurer and Chairman, of Lockgelly Violet FC, and came to a satisfactory arrangement with them with regards to your son William. I am now going fully into the matter of the job, at this end, for your Boy, and will report to you fuller particulars in the course of a few days. May I thank you for your kind hospitality to myself and my director, while at your home.

Rest assured that we will take very good care of your Boy – we will see that he has a homely place to live in, and we shall well look after his general welfare, while in Liverpool.

Yours Sincerely,

George Kay

Team Manager

PS. Kindly treat this matter very confidentially until I have everything fixed up for you.

WHEN THIS letter dropped through the letterbox of the Liddell family home, Billy was still studying for his final exams at Dunfermline High School. His life was about to be transformed more than he, his parents and George Kay could have ever expected.

Although this was dated in the summer of 1938, Billy did not get the opportunity to adorn the famous red shirt in an official match until 1946. Much of this is afforded to two major factors: firstly, Billy was only 16 when he made the move to Liverpool; and secondly, the Second World War was about to rip apart normal life for everyone and, on a much more trivial front, hugely disrupt the beginning of Billy's football career.

To rewind to before George Kay penned his letter to James Liddell, one man with links to Manchester United, Manchester City and Liverpool had a big hand in moving Billy to Merseyside. Sir Matt Busby played for Man City up to 1936 before signing for Liverpool. During a golfing trip with a former City team-mate, Alec Herd, Busby was informed that City were scouting a Lochgelly Violet starlet. The youngster was, of course, Willie Liddell; however, Billy's parents' insistence on an assurance of a professional football career before allowing him to leave Townhill discouraged Man City and several other rival clubs. Hearing of his talents, Busby was quick to alert his manager, George Kay.

Within a few weeks, Kay travelled to Scotland with Liverpool director Bill McConnell to meet the Liddells and persuade them that Liverpool was the place for Billy to go. The two made the five-hour journey by car. The combination of an assured professional contract, an apprenticeship as a chartered accountant in Liverpool and a good home for him to stay in, all partnered with £200 for Lochgelly, meant that it was an offer that was too good to resist.

Liverpool were obviously keen to get their man and that is all the family was after. If they were going to let their 16-year-old leave, they had to be sure that they found him the right club that had his best interests at heart. Fortunately for everyone involved, Liverpool and Liddell were the perfect fit. (Manchester Ciddell was nowhere near as catchy as Liddellpool either!)

The family must be afforded a lot of praise for ensuring that Billy had an accountancy string to his footballing bow. This, and the careful selection of club, meant that Billy had the best chance of success in Liverpool, regardless of his footballing fortunes. To have such supportive parents, on-field talent and a determined work ethic illustrates why he was so successful.

Nevertheless, George Kay did have to work to convince James and Montgomery, as Liverpool had a bad reputation as a city in the 1930s. In the words of Montgomery, she believed Liverpool was a 'den of iniquity'. The 1920s and 1930s were hard for Liverpool, a decline in traditional export commodities having led to nation-high levels of unemployment ahead of the Great Depression in the 1930s.

This combination of unemployment and loss of export trade jobs meant that a lot of people in the city were living in slums. To counteract this, the council pushed to rehouse 15 per cent of the city through an investment in local council housing.

This meant that towards the end of the 1930s Liverpool was recovering. There were now 30,000 new homes, the Queensway Tunnel provided a direct route from Liverpool to the Wirral, and new American-inspired architecture meant the city centre had been home to the 'Three Graces' (the Royal Liver Building, the Cunard Building and the Port of Liverpool Building) since the end of the 1910s.

Although the Liddells' Liverpool apprehension illustrated the public image of the city, the pre-Liddell Liverpool resurgence would have certainly helped ease their worries and secure Billy's signature. Kay and Liverpool were lucky that they managed to get their generational hero on board before the war further damaged the city's reputation and infrastructure.

Liverpool also owe a lot of thanks to the minister in Townhill, who helped ease Montgomery's concerns. The worry was not just Liverpool's poor reputation but the move from the rural bliss of Townhill to city life in Liverpool. The minister said, 'You'll be alright Gomrey,' his nickname for Mrs Liddell, and he was certainly right.

In the days before penthouse apartments for new players, Billy was housed with the widow of former Liverpool goalkeeper Ned Doig. Doig was an enigmatic and aged

Liverpool hero despite just four years at Anfield. He remains the oldest player to make his debut for the club, aged 37, and his final match when he was 41 means that he is the oldest player to ever play for the club as well. Despite his considerable age, he was dismayed when and at the means by which Liverpool informed him of the end of his career in 1908. They sent a postcard with a short message: 'Your services are no longer required'. Doig erupted into a fit of rage, smashing crockery and flipping tables. The unsanctimonious end to his career did not lead to a happy retirement as he died of Spanish flu in 1919, aged 53.

Whether Liverpool had felt guilty about their treatment of Doig, or more likely that the house he lived in was a club house, they allowed his widow and son to live in the property after his death. The same house that had received the blunt and disrespectful postcard in 1908 was about to house one of the future stars of the club as Liverpool arranged for Billy to live with Doig's widow, on Miriam Road in Anfield.

Billy was still only 16 and this provided him with a family home environment that would nurture his football and working life balance under the roof of a family well versed in early-20th-century football life.

Billy's biggest childhood football idol was his grandfather, and his simple words of advice were, 'When you go down to Liverpool, just be plain Billy Liddell and you'll get on.' In the nicest way possible, that is the best way to describe Billy. He kept his life plain, he worked hard in football, in accountancy and he went to church. His dedication and simplicity of life made him great and his grandfather was a huge inspiration on the rest of his career. Unfortunately for all involved, William was never able to witness Billy playing elite-level football but his early financial and moral support no doubt made Billy the player he was. He died in September 1939, aged 68. Billy had a motto: 'Play up, play up, and play the game' – the simplicity William preached stayed with him for his sporting life.

Although his parents had worried about Billy's safety in Liverpool, just months after his move south, the Liddell family narrowly escaped a tragedy in their family home. In January 1939, the fire brigade and police were called to save the Liddell and Stalker families following a near-fatal gas leak.

When Mrs Stalker and her two-year-old son Ian went to bed complaining of feeling sick, little thought was given to the strange smell that had invaded the family home that day. However, when Harry Stalker, the father, woke up in the middle of the night feeling sick and his legs buckling under him, he acted as quickly as he could to get the family to safety. He realised the smell was gas and threw open the windows, then went to wake up his 16-year-old twin daughters, who passed out as they got up from their beds. Harry managed to get two of his children out of the house and alert the Liddell family before passing out himself in an attempt to help his wife and two other children.

James Liddell was quick to help and get the rest of the Stalker family out of the house. He and Tom then ran to phone the police to come and help before James then passed out from the fumes. Montgomery was then able to alert the other neighbours before the police and fire brigade managed to attend.

It was found that a fractured gas main had caused the commotion and fortunately work began before anyone was seriously harmed. After receiving oxygen, all members of the Stalker and Liddell families were fine. Had it not been for Mr Stalker waking up and acting so quickly, who knows how many of both families could have died from the fumes. This certainly would have changed the course of Billy's life away from his supportive family. Had it occurred a few months earlier, he too could have been involved. Instead, he was lucky to be able to hear all of this scary news in a letter from his family while he was safe in Liverpool.

Despite not making his debut for the first team until after the war, Billy was enjoying life as a footballer and was quickly rewarded with a professional contract nine months after his Anfield arrival. His work life was progressing well too as he was holding down his role at Simon Jude and West, the company that handled the club's accounts, where he was studying to be an audit accountant with the firm. During his formative seasons, Billy only trained two days a week and worked for the other three, barring weekday matches and playing for Liverpool on the weekends.

Just a month shy of the beginning of the war, Billy was attracting the attention of George Kay and his staff. Local press reported following a match for the reserves that the 'Scottish lad, Liddell (who has grown almost out of recognition) was hearty and able in his approach work, and pulled the ball back in the approved style with good-length centres'. He was growing physically and was on the cusp of being ready to play for the Liverpool first team.

These early years of work and football also led to Billy meeting his future wife, Phyllis Farrance. The two met in 1939, just a few weeks before war was declared, and were courting for three years before their engagement in December 1942.

Billy used to write home to his family weekly and keep them abreast of his new life. His mother would remark that receiving a note from Bill was a 'red letter day'. As aforementioned, the war ruined so many of his peers' careers, but Billy was lucky that he had time to establish a life in Liverpool before the world was turned upside down.

The Men Who Put the Pool into Liddellpool - Alex South

One of the greatest opportunities this book has provided is speaking to some of the Liverpool players lucky enough to share the pitch, dressing room or football club with Billy Liddell. As much as this book has been written to tell the full story of Billy's life, to paint the full family portrait of the man, his football will always be the main aspect of his life and will draw the most attention. Who better then to tell the tale of what he was like as a team-mate than his Anfield colleagues and peers? In their own words, the story of Billy Liddell told by the people who put the pool in Liddellpool will be interspersed with chapters on his life story to further demonstrate the importance of the great Billy Liddell.

Alex South – Liverpool FC (1954–1956)

Billy was above me; he was lordly and was lauded by everybody. I never got on with Billy as I was misbehaving a lot in those days, I was a bit of a prat. I'm still a bit of a prat now! I was going through a funny period at that time.

I was only 22 when I was at Liverpool and Billy was the king of everyone. He was a magistrate, he sat on this and he sat on that. He was well behaved; he was too good to be true was Billy, but a great player ... a great, great player.

I only had six first-team games at Liverpool but one of them was at left-half and Billy was always a left-winger, of course, so consequently I was directly linked with Billy up the left flank. On one occasion the referee had accused me of something, and he gave a free kick. I threw the ball down the line, Billy ran after it. This was the sort he was. Billy ran all the way down 30 or 40 yards, picked the ball up, brought it all the way back and gave it to their player to take the free kick. They all booed me and cheered Billy, of course, because everybody loved him.

We were poles apart but, as is often the case with football, the 11 characters that play are all mixed up. Some are well behaved and some are prats. I was going through the prat period at that time. I have fond memories of Billy, he was such a good player, tremendous left foot.

I was way below his level of intelligence, according to Billy, and I had very little to do with him. When we were playing, we had no choice but to be together but if he'd have had his way, I would have been ten miles away! He was a very, very good player. I admired him. I never let him know that, but you couldn't help but admire Billy because he was such a good player. He couldn't half hit a ball with that left foot of his.

Billy was no sooner off the training pitch than he was in his civvies and he was off to do his private work. He was a pro, but he trained and then he was away. He was never hanging around doing useless things, he always had something worthwhile to do. Me, Barry Wilkinson and Roy Saunders, we would be at the dogs all the time, dog racing and birding and doing all untoward things. He was right and I was wrong. He was on too much of a pedestal, he never did anything wrong, which used to upset me! Not upset me but I used to think, is he absolutely perfect this guy?

I didn't envy him, I revered him. I looked up to Billy. The fans loved him, absolutely adored him. He was king there; he couldn't do wrong. Super player. If they ever picked an all-time Liverpool team, he would surely be in it. A gentleman, a scholar and a fine football player. He was some player was Billy. Once he got on a run with the ball, by Christ he took some stopping. He was like an express train down that wing!

3

The War and Wartime Football

IT IS hard to imagine that football could exist during the war. The six years that engulfed the globe in bloodshed also hosted a lot of unofficial football matches. Other than making it a nightmare to track individual players and their club-hopping traits, the era provided some unusual opportunities for the young men balancing football and fighting a war.

Despite it being such a short period between leaving Townhill and the war breaking out, Billy had done enough to impress George Kay and was on the brink of breaking into the first-team squad. Two months away in fact.

In September 1939, Britain and France declared war on Germany, commencing the start of the Second World War. In the December, an injury to Berry Nieuwenhuys saw a first-team debut for Billy against Preston North End at Anfield. He lined up alongside the man who helped bring him to Merseyside, Matt Busby, and his future manager, Phil Taylor.

Despite there being only 300 supporters in attendance, Billy shone on his first appearance with the first team. Reports of the match mentioned that 'Liddell showed great promise and was never beaten in this game, which deserved a 30,000 gate for the excellence of the football shown'. So impressive was the teenager's performance in the 1-0 loss that Billy was given his professional debut for Liverpool in the Western Division, two and a half weeks later.

The abovementioned clerical chaos caused by wartime football began almost immediately after the beginning of the war. Liverpool played three First Division matches in the 1939/40 campaign before football was formally halted, following the 50-mile travel limit that was introduced nationwide. This saw a transition into the leagues being regionalised with as many as ten separate divisions to work around the travel restrictions.

This, of course, took the real competitive edge from football in this period, not only because teams from the Third Division were now expected to compete with their First Division geographical neighbours, but because of wartime guests. Many players appeared for different clubs depending on where they were based at specific times during the war. The travel restrictions meant that the only way they could play a high standard of football was by appearing as wartime guests for other clubs.

Clubs used varying numbers of wartime guests. Liverpool had over 100 guest players during the war. The last-minute nature of the selections and lack of footage means that some of the names are debated but the number gives an idea of the amount of change there was in the squads during that time. Perhaps the most notable name to don the famous Liverpool red during the war was Bill Shankly. Both Billy Liddell and Bill Shankly lined up in the same Liverpool side to face Everton in a 4-1 victory at Anfield in May 1942.

Reading's Joffre Gulliver made 96 wartime appearances for Liverpool but has no official Liverpool appearances to his name, so he will be remembered as a player who did not play for the club. To put his contribution into perspective, his wartime appearance tally is just 14 fewer league matches than Luis Suárez played for the club. This illustrates how much of each player's career was robbed from them during the war.

Players such as Billy Liddell, Berry 'Nivvy' Nieuwenhuys and Tommy Lawton were so unlucky that their football careers were significantly interrupted by the war. When the Liverpool players were compared to previous Anfield legends Ernie Blenkinsop, Tommy Lucas, Jock McNab, Gordon Hodgson and Elisha Scott, it was hard for them as they lost so much of their career and could never challenge the prestige of the previous players.

Billy too was subject to the wartime football merry-go-round. Although the early period of the war allowed him the opportunity to break into the first team at Liverpool, he was soon sent around the world on his football travels. He represented Dunfermline Athletic, Hearts, Chelsea,

Linfield, Cambridge Town and Toronto Scottish during the war.

Although it has been said that it seems unfair that players were not accredited the appearances and goals they racked up during the war, the constant changing of teams and league reformations was, of course, a blockade to fair and consistent competition. However, it seems glaringly unfair that this whole period of football is wiped from the record books today.

Both players and supporters were putting their lives at risk by just attending the matches, never mind their actions away from the football stadiums for the rest of their week. Their love for football was worth the risk for all involved. The clubs had to rely on their historic neighbouring rivals to keep football alive and to provide a distraction spectacle to the loyal supporters who turned up. The decision to ignore all wartime football and sweep it under the carpet seems very disrespectful to all involved.

To further understand the decision to allow this to happen, the league changes should be analysed more closely. The split to ten divisions in 1939 saw Liverpool placed in the Western League. This lasted for a year until the country was split into the Northern and Southern Regional League with 34 teams in each division. The following year, the Northern and Southern Leagues were split into two, meaning there were now four divisions for the country. In 1942, more change saw the country now split into three divisions and each division was split in two, Liverpool being in the West League of the Northern Regional League. This lasted until 1945 when the league reverted to two divisions following the end of the war, but it was still classed as wartime football as the league had already started prior to peacetime. This all coincided with the Football League War Cup, which also took place throughout the war. The FA Cup then returned for the 1945/46 campaign, following the end of the war.

The complex structure has helped to keep this period in historical insignificance as it is a very complicated period of football. The lack of, and untrustworthy, sources means that wartime football will never be correctly remembered or respected. Nevertheless, it was six years of Billy Liddell's career just as he was on the cusp of breaking into the Liverpool first team.

He had made his first appearance for the first team in the Anfield friendly match against Preston and he was continuing to impress. He was then handed his first competitive match during a 7-3 win against Crewe Alexandra, where he was competing alongside fellow youngsters Len Carney and George Leadbitter but proved to be the shining light. His performance was lauded in the press: 'The star performer was Liddell, a wing-forward not yet 18, and played at outside-left to give a most promising display, his ball control and sense of positioning being features.' Billy's first competitive performance also brought with it a goal inside two minutes.

This fast-track to the first team was largely due to the absence of his elder team-mates who had immediately joined the war effort. Billy was not called up by the RAF until 1943, so he used this three and a half year period of early access to the team to his benefit. He was playing with some very experienced players, such as Matt Busby, every week and experiencing large crowds and exciting atmospheres at the same time.

Billy was also able to experience several Merseyside derbies during the war. The young Scot was certainly out to impress against the Toffees in 1941, so eager in fact that when Berry Nieuwenhuys sent a cross in, Billy not only met the ball with his head but subsequently the goalpost. In the days before correct concussion protocol, Billy seemed to be on the wrong end of more than his fair share of collisions. However, it was deemed unmanly to not just get up and play on. He was certainly a fearless competitor, with strength beyond his stature. However, his battle in later life with dementia, which will be discussed later, can only lead to the investigation and highlighting of every small incident like this one against Everton when he was just 18.

Billy's fledgling Liverpool career was attracting attention from further afield. The Scotland selectors were soon calling George Kay to ask whether Billy could partake in a wartime international match. This was to be his international debut against none other than the old rivals, England.

Scotland produced an emphatic performance, with the 5-4 scoreline not fairly representing the gulf between the two neighbouring nations. The fallout from the match in the press was heavily centred around the exciting Billy Liddell on his maiden international call-up, alongside the influential performances of Bill Shankly and Matt Busby. Billy's performance was acclaimed:

MAESTRO LIDDELL

Liddell for instance. Carol Levis has nothing on the S.F.A. when it comes to discoveries. Ten minutes was sufficient for this boy to play himself into these critical, hard-beating Hampden hearts. He took the equaliser with a lovely timed header. But it was the say he had in the second goal which put him in the Maestro class. Liddell did the spadework and (Ephraim 'Jock') Dodds did the finishing for what must be one of the greatest goals Hampden has ever seen. The outstripping of the defence, the quick pass with the 'wrong' foot, and then Dodds's glorious first-timer. What a goal!

Of the five goals Scotland scored, Billy scored one and assisted two on his first Scotland appearance. He proved that he was not just a stopgap player for a wartime international, he was here to stay and wanted to be a mainstay of the Scottish side.

Busby was not only pivotal in the match, but he was a constant beacon of guidance playing behind Billy on the day, advising him with the simple words of 'just play your usual club game, Willie'. This was also the first opportunity that Billy's parents had to watch their son and they were immensely proud to see their boy light up Hampden. Busby went to meet them before the match and assured them 'your laddie is a natural footballer and can also keep his head'.

Billy's parents had not been able to see him making his name in Liverpool Reserves so this provided them with a rare opportunity to watch him play after he had left home. James would listen when Billy played for Liverpool but could go and watch him for the home Scotland matches. For both of Billy's parents to be at this match illustrates how important this day was to the family. They were so pleased and proud of Billy; the whole wider family still supported their home teams but also became and remain fanatical Liverpool supporters because of their new family connection.

Billy asked all his team-mates to sign his programme after the match as a memento of his first Scotland call-up. He was still so young but had performed ahead of his 20 years; however, just under a year later he was due to be called up for the RAF, so his Liverpool and Scotland opportunities became sparser.

* * *

In April 1941, Billy enlisted at RAF Padgate, where he trained and was given his service number 1523547. Padgate, a suburb of Warrington (just outside of Liverpool), was also host to fellow Scottish and Liverpool legend Bill Shankly. Shankly left Padgate in 1940 ahead of his RAF war efforts so the two did not encounter each other.

Billy was so desperate to continue his football that he snuck out of Padgate to play for Liverpool, and despite being in Warrington for training, he still managed to play a further eight matches and score four goals for Liverpool before the 1940/41 season ended.

Billy had applied to be a pilot for the RAF, but he was asked to be a navigator due to his mathematical ability. So, he was a navigator in a Lancaster bomber during a period that he liked to remain very private. It was 18 months of his life during which he travelled the world and was not directly involved in fighting but was transporting troops away from the battlefield. It was certainly a dangerous proposition for him, during which his physique and intelligence were beneficial.

Despite his mathematical talents, the fact that Billy was selected as a navigator was of much amusement to the Liddell family. Billy was renowned within the family for having a terrible sense of direction. Rena, his younger sister, recalls that the family used to point up at planes flying past their house during the war and remark that it was Billy flying the wrong way!

During trips to Scotland in later life, Billy would be driving the family round in circles but never admit to his mistakes. Being such a quiet and softly spoken man, his one-word answers of 'yes' or 'no' would be the only response they could muster in return for asking why they had driven past the same place five times during the 20th minute of a five-minute journey.

Billy was not the only Liddell to join the war effort, as Tom and Campbell were both in the Army. Tom was later injured in the D-day landings, which affected his hearing. Campbell was also injured during the war, causing him to return home. The two were not in the same squadron but they met up during a tour in Egypt during the war.

Their father, James, now an insurance agent, could not partake fully in the war effort due to his age and his ill health at the time. In fact, he was only a few years from his death from hypertension pneumoconiosis cardiac failure. Put simply, his heart was becoming increasingly blocked, presumably by the thick soot and ash from his time down the mines. The poor health and safety standards of mining were all but a death warrant for James. So, he remained at home with Montgomery, Alastair, George and Rena.

Billy being in the RAF meant that he was away from all his family throughout the war, but his football made him a popular man wherever he was based and provided him with a lot of football experience. He was fortunate to meet some good friends, new and old, during his time with the RAF.

Bill Tracey was a fellow navigator who grew up with Billy and his brothers in Townhill. Bill was a flight engineer who was posted in Lincoln and Blackpool. He went to visit Billy while he was in Blackpool's RAF Remedial Centre as Billy had suffered a broken leg in a kickabout, which fortunately did not affect his future career, despite ruling him out of a Scotland wartime friendly.

The two Bills remained great friends after the war, Tracey moving to Liverpool not long afterwards. They would have great days in the Liddell household reminiscing about school days, Townhill, Dunfermline, calling themselves the 'Flying Scots', and cooking some Scottish classics. There was always the smell of baking 'cut and come again cake' and 'melting moments' biscuits, all childhood favourites of the Liddell clan. Scottish afternoon tea with scotch pancakes, cake and biscuits seemed to be celebrated most days.

Tracey's son, Ian, would call Billy and Phyllis Uncle and Aunty and had a great relationship with the Liddell family. Billy often gave Ian programmes and memorabilia and Ian idolised his adopted uncle. It is perhaps best to allow Ian's words to describe their relationship:

> He had an absolutely winning smile, which could light up a room. He was so very modest and so very humble, quietly spoken but with an immense presence and charisma which was palpable. It is oft said of many that 'we shall never see his like again!'

but I do feel that in the case of Wully Liddell, this may indeed be a truth. A true 'gentleman' in every sense of the word, and a lovely Christian man, whom it was my immense privilege to know, and moreover to be able to call 'friend'.

The pilot that Billy navigated was named George Telford, who went on to become Billy's best man at his wedding. They would enjoy playing and chatting about football together, although Billy was much more talented. The two remained in touch after the war, and Billy and Phyllis would travel to Edinburgh to visit George and his wife Joan, often exchanging visits. The Telfords married in Garston in Liverpool, Billy's younger twin siblings Rena and George being page boy and girl for the day. The two families spent lots of time together playing cricket and football in later life.

Billy's official role was in the Navigator Pathfinder Force, RAF Bomber Command and Coastal Command from 1942 to 1946. The navigators were the cream in the Pathfinders, and the air operator's certificate meant that, besides being a brilliant pilot, Billy and the rest of his squadron were Master Navigators.

He was proud of his time as a navigator and kept his uniform for the rest of his life, despite never wanting to discuss or dwell on his service. It is fair to assume that he would have experienced his fair share of heartache during the war, but this was a different time when bottling up emotions and painful memories was as much encouraged as it was the norm. He was always a man of few words but the fact that his family and friends know next to nothing of his time in the RAF illustrates his method of dealing with that period of his life.

Billy not only held a prestigious role but was also awarded the War Medal 1939–1945 and the 1939–1945 Star. The War Medal was given to all men and women who served full-time in the armed forces for at least 28 days during the war. The Star was awarded for RAF crew who had served over 60 days of service outside Britain.

These foreign tours followed Billy's training at Padgate. He was moved to St John's Wood in Westminster in late 1942, which is when he guested for Chelsea. Billy was stationed with the Chelsea quartet Len Goulden, Dick Spence, Joe Payne and manager Walter Winterbottom, the future England manager, who convinced Billy to turn out for Chelsea on several occasions, one of which was an RAF XI vs Police match in January 1943. Billy played as a Chelsea player for the match.

Billy then moved briefly to Cambridge, where he represented Cambridge Town before flying to Canada for further navigation training. While there he was provided the opportunity to play for Toronto Scottish. Due to the seemingly stricter clerical rules in Canada, Billy had to use a pseudonym of Bill Tanner (in a surprising act of Liddell dishonesty) to be able to play for the Scottish expat side. He was just so desperate to play the game he loved. After scoring two goals in ten minutes, it became obvious that Tanner may not be who he seemed!

After eight months in Canada, Billy was delighted to discover that he was to be based in Perth, just 25 miles from home in Townhill. This allowed him the chance to represent some Scottish sides, such as Hearts in August 1943 against a select RAF XI.

One positive opportunity the war did provide for Billy was to represent his hometown team, Dunfermline Athletic. He was so pleased to be able to play for the side he had grown up watching. His family had witnessed the rivalry between Dunfermline and Cowdenbeath for years and now he could be part of his team.

This was a great thrill for all the family and especially James, who was a loyal 'Pars' supporter. The Dunfermline locals were delighted to welcome the local star back, not just because of his birthplace, but because he was a great player. Billy was pivotal in a 5-1 victory over East Fife in November 1944 and he was described as lifting a depression on Dunfermline with his presence and performance. He scored two and the Liddell family was quick to collect local news clippings of a historic day where his performance was described:

> The psychological effect which this player produced
> on his team-mates was, in my opinion, an elevating

one. His presence at a time when they were 'down in the dumps' acted like a tonic, and the response was no half-hearted one. Space will not permit to enumerate all the strong points in Willie's game, and I will content myself by saying he had that touch of class which goes to make international players.

Billy continued to dazzle his home supporters and make his family proud with several great performances for Dunfermline. Another came in a 7-2 away victory against Dundee United in December, where he again inspired a great team performance, scoring a free kick and being an all-round menace from the left wing. He had a seemingly telepathic link with Jacky Hunter on the day, who scored five goals, Billy assisting two.

It is clear the ability that Billy had across these wartime appearances, as he seemed to score in nearly every match he played and normally had an assist or two. Much is made of statistics and numbers in today's game, and Billy's goal contributions were through the roof, particularly during the wartime period. Assists were not regularly recorded then, so it is hard to know his exact numbers for his career, but his influence in front of goal was phenomenal.

So impressive were Billy's performances that he was again selected for Scotland in a wartime friendly sandwiched between the two prior-mentioned Dunfermline matches, in late November 1944. In all, Billy played in eight international wartime matches, scoring three goals. He also lined up for a Scotland XI against an RAF side, scoring two goals at Hillsborough in front of 45,000 spectators. He played alongside Liverpool team-mates Jim Harley, Willie Fagan and captain Matt Busby, with all three men on the scoresheet.

Billy also had time to represent Linfield during the latter stages of the war, when he was unable to help former Liverpool great Elisha Scott, who managed Belfast Celtic and had asked Billy to play. Without doubt it was breaking into the Liverpool team, representing his country and, above all, playing for his home team that defined the wartime matches for Billy Liddell.

* * *

It does feel I have given the significantly trivial side of the war more time and analysis. In truth, Billy would have preferred not to have dwelled on his time in the RAF. It was something he wanted to do and was proud of it, but never something he wanted to discuss. That does not mean it should be ignored; he was a brave man in an era of heroes. All the men and women who were involved in the war effort deserve never-ending praise.

What Billy could also provide was a release and a break from the harsh reality of war life by playing football. He was certainly doing it for himself as much as anyone else; he was football mad and loved playing the game. However, what he and so many other footballers did during this period was amazing. They all turned up in great numbers across the country in front of tens of thousands of fans. Their morale-boosting displays would no doubt have helped the war effort for all those lucky enough to be in attendance.

Billy grew from a boy to a man during the war. He was 17 at the outbreak and by the time the first full Football League season returned to Liverpool he was 24. He had changed so much, from the young boy in a giant RAF hat that engulfed his head, to the physically developed young man of the mid-1940s. He never mentioned that he felt the war had robbed some of his best years; he was so humble and unassuming that he would never view this experience in any hint of a selfish way. He was happy to be able to play the sport he loved, write home to his parents and write to his new fiancée Phyllis. She too was involved with the war effort with the RAF. She was based in Altrincham, which meant she could still regularly visit home in Liverpool, continuing her concerts and dancing in the city with her famously long legs.

This was a significant period of Billy's life and set him up for the next 15 years of football that he had ahead of him. Much is made of his loyalty to Liverpool, as it should be, but it is perhaps also wise to view his career in the context of the war as well. He was given the opportunity to represent at least eight different teams during this time and, of course, the possibility of him remaining a one-club man was out of his hands as club-hopping was a normal action of every player of this era. However, this allowed Billy the experience of football around Britain, in his hometown and abroad, and perhaps removed the air of mystery and intrigue over a potential move in later years. All this was in conjunction with the real risk and danger that his fiancée and several family members could have been killed during the war. It is fair to assume that the romance of a move away from Liverpool was quashed and the true importance of a consistent, safe, happy and healthy family life became of prominent importance. The events in his family over the next few years also meant that his bond with Liverpool grew stronger.

On the pitch, Billy's first wartime season saw him make 16 appearances and score nine goals. From the 1940/41 season up to 1957/58 he played at least 30 matches a season, other than the three years he was with the RAF. Some players need an element of luck to get into a side. A world war cannot be considered lucky but it did allow Billy the opportunity to bed himself into the team as a young player, and when official football resumed, he was ready to hit the ground running.

The Men Who Put the Pool into Liddellpool – Keith Burkinshaw

Keith Burkinshaw – Liverpool FC (1953–1957)

He was the best player by a good bit at Liverpool at that time, on the odd occasion they would pick me to look after the kit. He was a terrific player and of course a Scottish international and I was in awe of him all the time I was there. In those days, you didn't really get to know the older players as well as you might. Let's face it, there was about 50-odd pros, all professionals at the club so you wouldn't get really friendly with the older players.

He was such a big figure; he must have brought a lot to Liverpool as a football club because when he played for Scotland he was pretty good as well. The club was struggling badly at times then. He was always okay with me in training; there were quite a few players around his age, so he spent most of his time with them, people like Ray Lambert and Alan A'Court.

He wasn't a guy who would be shouting and bawling. He was such a big figure, and I would have loved to have seen him in his early twenties. There were a lot of players that went through the war and then afterwards found themselves in the first team. He was a strong-bodied fella, quite quick. He was the one that scored the goals at Liverpool. He was outstanding from that point of view.

He was a player that other players looked up to, the most influential player at Liverpool while I was there with regard to the winning and losing of games because he was the one who scored the most number of goals and he had a big effect on the team.

4

Winning the League 1946/47

THE TITLE of the chapter, and some prior Liddell knowledge, may perhaps ruin the conclusion of this famous campaign. Nevertheless, it was a hugely significant and sadly solitary moment of silverware for Billy. We enter this campaign following the fallout of the war, the players having been able to spend the best part of a year recovering, returning home and mentally preparing themselves for the resumption of football.

George Kay, and every one of his contemporary football managers, had the prospect of juggling new players who had established themselves during the war, established pre-war players who were now six years older, and the already aged players now at the very end of their careers. It was a truly thankless and seemingly impossible task.

The supporters were public with their worries, one writing a letter to the *Liverpool Echo* stating: 'There is no benefit to be derived from this oft-recurring familiarity of old players who have never been good enough to represent our loyal gang of followers. No club has a better following, no club is served up with such fruitless result.'

The clubs would have been financially struggling, despite wartime matches having provided large gates. They would have no doubt felt an element of responsibility to help players and their families return to normality. Liverpool, it is fair to assume, dealt with this predicament the best and wanted to attack the first Football League season since the war. They did so with an unprecedented pre-season tour of North America.

Before we board the boat to the US, it seems like a good time to analyse post-wartime football tactics. Before tactics and philosophies such as 4-4-2, tiki-taka, total football and 4-3-3, was the 'W'. It is a bizarrely attacking-looking formation when viewed through the prism of modern football tactics. The best way to describe the set-up is perhaps visually:

11	10	9	8	7
Outside-left	*Inside-left*	*Centre-forward*	*Inside-right*	*Outside-right*
	6	5	4	
	Left-half	*Centre-half*	*Right-half*	
	3		2	
	Left-back		*Right-back*	
		1		
		Goalkeeper		

This was pretty much the universal formation used across English football. The illustration should help better depict the positions of each notable player that may be discussed from this point onwards. The right/left-half, outside-right/left and inside-right/left positions have all become redundant in today's football terminology. Much like with soccer, these are terms from a football era gone by.

The numbers are also significant, this being a period before specific squad numbers were assigned to an individual player. In modern football, numbers from 1 to 99 are used, but this was not the case in Billy's era and the number merely signified what position you were playing. The shirts themselves were recycled for several seasons before being retired as training shirts until they were binned when all but threadbare, making any club shirt from this era incredibly rare.

This analysis also helps show the development of Billy over his career. He predominantly played as an outside-left, famously donning the number 11 shirt for Liverpool and Scotland over many years. He built strong relationships with two influential left-halves during his career: initially mentored by Matt Busby, and then, as friends and team-mates, he and Bob Paisley had a great bond. Billy also had spells as an inside-left and outside- or inside-right; however, his wing play was a huge part of his game. Beating defenders with electric pace and grace, he would then either cross to perfection or take the ball into the box and unleash a lethal shot. He was predominantly left-footed but was more than able with both feet. The force he could unleash with either foot was as potent as his heading ability. He was neither tall nor small, standing at six feet, but his physique, leap and power made him the complete attacking package.

As his body aged, Billy was moved to centre-forward. Much like the development of Cristiano Ronaldo, the goalscoring ability was still present, but his reducing speed meant that he became more potent from the centre of the pitch.

This is also a good time to mention that Billy represented Liverpool in every outfield position on the pitch. Being a period before substitutions, whenever a player was injured and incapable of continuing on the pitch, there was no option but to reshuffle the players available. Billy's physicality and fitness made him versatile, meaning he could fill in at right- or left-half or right- or left-back, as well as his heading ability and strength making him competent at centre-half.

In fact, if it had not been for Ronnie Moran, Billy would have completed the 'play in every position' feat that not many have had the chance to achieve. Away to Derby County in 1957, goalkeeper Tommy Younger was injured following a hefty kick to his back, meaning he was unable to continue in goal. Liddell and Moran both offered their services to manager Phil Taylor to deputise in goal, as the decision was made that keeper Younger would go up front and away from the action due to him barely being able to walk. Moran was favoured to play in goal as Younger was being pushed upfield, and Billy was given the task of filling in for Moran at left-back. The move was far from successful as Younger was ineffectual and Moran conceded a Derby winner with under ten minutes remaining.

Billy being the complete footballing package meant that it is fair to assume he could have had a career in any position. No doubt his school rugby skills would have benefited his ability to catch the ball if he had ever wanted to transition into a goalkeeper full-time!

The conclusion of the previous chapter saw the end of the war, Billy returning to Liverpool as the first post-war season was teed up. It must be noted that the war ended in September 1945 and the maiden First Division match in peacetime was in August 1946. This was because the final wartime season had already begun before the end of the war and allowed all clubs time to get their house in order.

Billy returned to Liverpool and played in 28 post-war, 'wartime' fixtures, 20 at outside-left, eight as an outside-right, and he scored 15 goals. This was a more than acceptable return for a winger and it must always be remembered that his assists were not consistently tracked. However, towards the end of the campaign his chances started to dry up as he was competing for a place in the side with Harry Eastham, Bob Priday and Berry Nieuwenhuys. This reduced access to the team illustrated that the following season would be tough for Billy, despite his excellent return when called upon. However, a lot of his absences were RAF-related as they still requested soldiers to return to finish training and/ or complete dismemberment and dispersal protocol.

One other major event that occurred prior to the 1946/47 campaign was Billy's competitive debut for Liverpool in an FA Cup tie away to Chester. Due to the lengthy gap since another competitive match, he was not alone in making his debut on that day as seven others (Kevin Baron, Laurie Hughes, Ray Lambert, Harry Wheeler, Bob Priday, Fred Finney and Bob Paisley) also played their first match. However, Liddell was the only debut man to score on the occasion, his half-hour strike helping Liverpool to a 2-0 victory on a day the *Cheshire Observer Newspaper* described him as 'the star of the Liverpool attack'.

Billy made one more FA Cup appearance that season before Liverpool were knocked out 5-2 over two legs by Bolton Wanderers. The FA Cup had been revived post-war as a way of introducing competitive football again, Derby County winning the cup in front of nearly 100,000 supporters in a gala Wembley occasion. It does again seem unfair, though, that this competition is deemed to have been competitive in a season of wartime matches and friendlies.

Nevertheless, Billy's friendly wartime league and FA Cup debuts had now all been achieved, and he was certainly a 24-year-old established member of the Liverpool team that was about to head to North America ahead of the 1946/47 season. The menu of steaks, maple syrup and orange juice were far away from food-rationed Britain but also far from Liddell.

* * *

The RAF recalled Billy following the end of the previous campaign, meaning that he missed the club's maiden journey to North America. However, the summer did provide him time to marry his fiancée, Phyllis Farrance. In July 1946, the Liddell family made the trip south to witness the first wedding in their family. RAF friend George Telford was best man to Billy, with twins Rena and George assisting as flower girl and page boy respectively. Phyllis lived in Garston and the two were married in Garston Park Methodist Church. The whole Liddell family came down, including aunties and uncles, to celebrate the wedding. It was a very good day and the only occasion on which many, including James Liddell, made their visit to Liverpool.

The rest of the squad was on the North American tour, which was so successful that the team ultimately returned Stateside the following summer, when Liddell could finally attend. While on the trip, he shared letters with his parents, and Montgomery wrote: 'I believe you Bill when you say that you have been homesick, for there is no place like home and with the one you love. But never mind son, it will be all the sweeter when you get back. Have a good time, it will do you good for you were needing it.'

Updating Billy on family life, his mother commented: 'Dad has just got back from the bowling green, he is still coughing away and I am wanting him to go to the doctor but he will not hear of it.' Advice that James really should have taken from his wife as the long-term effects of his mining were getting a firmer grip of him. Montgomery signed off with: 'P.S. keep up the good work and lots of luck, hope you keep winning.'

The next letter on this trip was sent from James and picked straight back up with 'glad to see you are still keeping up the winning vein'. He passed on a request from Alastair for 'a good pair of swimming pants'. The squad visited the US and Canada and Billy brought back gifts for his family, which was unusual, as it was not something he had done while on Scotland away matches or during the war. The gift of chewing gum was also unfamiliar to the Liddells, who had not seen it before. He also brought back some clothes for George, a dress for Rena and T-shirts for the rest of the Liddell lads. Perhaps the end of the war and the hope of a new family he was building with Phyllis implored Billy to treat his Townhill family, as well as the obvious feeling of being homesick that Montgomery had commented on.

It was not all steak and chewing gum for those on the 1946 North America trip though; there was also some football played. Bill McConnell, the director who attended Billy's family home in 1938, was the architect of the trip. He saw the potential health benefits available to the players in the prosperous and ration-less nation. George Kay was quickly won over so the players and staff made plans for their eight-week expedition, leaving four days after their final wartime match.

The club benefited a lot from their trip to North America and it really was pioneering. They had access to floodlights, or 'night lights' as George Kay labelled them, against the American league champions, Baltimore Americans. Anfield did not have floodlights until 1957 but the directors were certainly impressed with the ability to play evening matches under them. The 1957 debut of floodlights at Anfield was played in the tester event, the Floodlight Challenge Cup. Everton were welcomed to an illuminated Anfield and Billy scored two in a 3-2 derby win.

When they all returned to Liverpool after the tour, the stark difference between the prosperous post-war US and a heavily bombed Liverpool was worrying. After weeks of limitless food and relative elegance, they returned to earth with a bang. The squad was still without Liddell, Cyril Sidlow and Ray Lambert, and these were the days before their soon-to-be-built training complex, Melwood.

This meant that training was completed at Anfield, therefore the grass was always ruined halfway through the season. When it was so bad (frozen, waterlogged or boggy) that training could not be completed, the players would run up and down the steps of the Kop to keep fit or train in the gym situated under the Main Stand. It was clear that a training ground was needed, and it did come in the 1950s, but for now the players had to cope with a damaged Anfield pitch plus broken plumbing and no running water. The pictures of the squad pre-season show the state of the training equipment, the shirts misshapen, and the pitch already looking boggy. It was testament to the trainers that Liverpool were physically fit and happy to endure these poor training standards.

The traditional Liverpool season curtain raiser was the First Team in red, against the Reserves in white. The match was often billed as the Probables vs the Possibles, the expected first XI players against those after their places for the upcoming campaign. There would also be a marathon run by the A, B and C team players, with the winner getting the opportunity to come on as a substitute for the final stages of the match.

Billy was expected to impress, whichever side he was selected for, and to establish his place for the upcoming season. However, an impromptu England vs Scotland charity match in support of the Burnden Park disaster (a human crush that occurred in March 1946 at Bolton Wanderers' stadium, resulting in the deaths of 33 people and injuring hundreds), a no doubt noble cause, which illustrated Billy's Scottish standing, further disrupted his delayed return from the RAF. Not only in terms of missing the match, but from the thigh injury he picked up, which ruled him out of the first two matches of the season.

* * *

The 1946/47 campaign was set to be a very dramatic one for George Kay's Liverpool side as he orchestrated a first top-flight title in nearly 25 years, and a fifth overall, with the average home gate topping 40,000 for the first time in the club's history. The season began with a 1-0 win at Sheffield United but then a defeat by the same scoreline at home to Middlesbrough.

Kay was keen to ensure his side bounced back against Chelsea, and September brought the West Londoners to Anfield for what would be remembered as a milestone moment, with an amazing scoreline, in Liddell and Liverpool history. The Chelsea side boasted former Everton forward Tommy Lawton in their ranks. The Liverpool boss made four changes: out went Cyril Sidlow, Eddie Spicer, Len Carney and Bob Priday; in came Charlie Ashcroft, Willie Fagan, Bob Paisley and Billy Liddell.

Bob and Billy had both signed pro contracts with the club back in 1939 and went on to have immeasurable success. This was their official competitive debut proper, a remarkable amount of time to wait to pull on the jersey for real.

No one in the 50,000-strong crowd could have anticipated the role that both men would go on to play for the club. Kay, though, had seen enough to hand them their starts, and those present were in for a treat with no fewer than 11 goals scored at a packed Anfield. The debutant duo were afforded credit in the post-match *Liverpool Echo* report, which began with the headline 'Liddell and Paisley Transformed Liverpool Attack', Billy no doubt benefiting from his wartime playing days with Chelsea as extra intel for him and the team prior to kick-off.

The home side's display was electric, with Billy scoring the first goal in the second minute directly from a corner. Bill Jones's brace and a Willie Fagan goal put Liverpool four up at half-time. During the break, reported the *Echo*, a 'number of youths got into the ground by scaling the wall on Anfield Road', while thousands more waited outside Anfield listening.

Jack Balmer scored soon after the break and Billy got a second, meaning that Liverpool were 6-0 up after only 50 minutes. An off-the-ball collision while scoring his second stalled Billy's performance for the rest of the match – another example of his persevering through injury, although this time thankfully no harm was caused to his head. But although Billy had been superb, the Anfield faithful could also see that it was Paisley who was crafting his chances.

It was not until the 55th minute that Chelsea scored their first goal, but they soon made up for lost time, finding the net three times more in quick succession: Len Goulden and Jimmy Argue efforts combined with a double from Alex Machin. It was now 6-4 with still 20 minutes left on the clock! Nerves, injury and fatigue seemed to have played a part for the Liverpool side, but as the visitors pressed forward, the hosts scored again through Fagan. It ended 7-4.

The police on duty could not contain the swarms of young supporters who ran on to the pitch to mob their heroes at the final whistle. They had just witnessed sensational debuts from a duo who would become Liverpool legends in their own right, their careers having an impact upon the football club that very few have ever come near to matching.

A week on, forward Albert Stubbins joined from Newcastle United for £13,000 – the final piece in a title-challenging jigsaw. He would go on to score 83 goals in 178 appearances for Liverpool. The Tyneside-born forward had a shot so venomous that he broke the wrist of Leeds United's John Hodgson that season when the keeper saved his penalty. His famous diving header in the snow against Birmingham City, following a superbly delivered free kick by Billy, will be long remembered for the thunderous finish and the fact that he cut both knees open after landing on the icy Anfield turf.

The Chelsea match was only a glimpse to Liverpool supporters, who had yet to properly witness Billy, but it illustrated what was to come that season and for the rest of his Liverpool days. He won the supporters over with his ability, eye for the goal and anticipation. When he got the ball, they knew he was going to run at the full-back and create something. Nine times out of ten he would go past him and get his cross in. He was one of those players that when the ball dropped to his feet it would lift the fans and there was a palpable feeling of growing Anfield anticipation.

Next up was a crushing defeat to an old Anfield friend. Matt Busby, the new Manchester United manager, welcomed his former team-mates and protégés Liddell, Paisley and Phil Taylor to Old Trafford. Busby had verbally agreed to join the Liverpool staff with a view to working his way up to the managerial position in the future, but he was later offered the United managerial job outright and swiftly took the role. The prospect of a Liverpool staff hosting Shankly, Paisley and Busby sounds like the recipe for endless Anfield trophies or quarrels, but safe to say that all three men did well with their choices, regardless. Liverpool had tried to host a testimonial for Busby's Liverpool contribution but United did not want him to play, so it never came to fruition.

Billy was again to miss out due to RAF commitments. It brought another disappointing display without Billy as Busby's first-ever 'babes' easily dispatched five goals against a hapless Liverpool. Billy's importance to the team was becoming clear. George Kay had given him every opportunity to play but injury and RAF commitments were holding him back. However, come mid-September Billy was unleashed and now had the potent Albert Stubbins to link up with – a title-winning partnership was born.

Two goals in successive October matches, both away, to Grimsby Town and Middlesbrough, meant that Billy had started the season with six goals in six matches. This remarkable start did two things: firstly, it showed that the supporters and George Kay were right to trust him; and secondly, it made it all the more unbelievable that in the following 34 matches that season, he only scored two more goals.

It is hard to fathom why this happened, as goalscoring had been a part of wartime Liddell and the future Liddellpool poster boy, but his early Liverpool days were not as goal-drenched, although he went on to be the top goalscorer for seven out of eight seasons from 1949 to 1957 for the Reds. This early dearth of goals cannot be described as a dip in form, as Billy was a winger and his job was to beat the man and get the ball into the box. He grew into his role of goalscorer as he matured and his importance to the team grew.

Albert Stubbins had just been signed for £13,000, which was the club's record transfer fee and remained so for 15 years, the same season that Billy retired. The acquisition of a player signed for such a fee illustrates the importance the board placed on Stubbins, and his role in the team was to score the goals. This still being a time when the board of directors selected the team, their selection and instructions were centred around Billy feeding Stubbins the ball, and it worked. Billy was a mainstay of a side where Stubbins scored over 25 goals in his first two seasons, finishing as the club's top scorer in both.

* * *

By December 1946, Liverpool sat two points behind Wolverhampton Wanderers, having played a match less. It is important to note here that this was in an era of two points for a win and one for a draw. The title race was heating up between the teams that were to take the race to the bitter end of the campaign: Liverpool, Wolves (captained by Ellesmere Port-born Stan Cullis), Busby's United, and Billy's English counterpart Stanley Matthews's Stoke City (before his transfer to Blackpool in May 1947).

In light of the structural chaos caused by the Blitz bombing on Merseyside, housing was at an all-time low. Liverpool Football Club had invested in a big trip to North America and their record signing Stubbins. They now moved to help some of the players building young families and in dire need of housing. They did this by purchasing six new-build semi-detached club houses on Westfield Avenue and Greystone Road in Broadgreen, less than 15 minutes from Anfield by car.

This meant that Billy and Phyllis had a place of their own, alongside the budding families of Willie Fagan, Phil Taylor, Cyril Done, Eddie Spicer, Albert Stubbins and later Bob Paisley. The club should be afforded a lot of praise for their post-war lavishness. This was a wise investment, though, as they now had a further incentive to attract the next Stubbins as housing was of such high importance in post-war Britain.

Perhaps buoyed by this housing news, Billy was on the scoresheet against Sunderland in a match where he was again concussed. Treacherous conditions saw the pitch turn all but

Billy Liddell in November 1949

Billy Liddell shaking hands with King George VI prior to kick-off for the 1950 FA Cup Final

Billy Liddell and the Scotland national team, October 1952

Billy Liddell and the Great Britain squad, August 1955

Billy Liddell in training with Liverpool in July 1957

Billy Liddell in September 1957

Billy Liddell vs. Wolves December 1946

Billy Liddell August 1949

Billy Liddell vs. Fulham September 1950

Billy Liddell vs. Leyton Orient, February 1958

Billy Liddell vs Exeter City in the FA Cup, January 1950

Billy Liddell Scotland vs. England April 1953

Billy Liddell vs. Manchester City February 1956

Billy Liddell vs. Blackburn Rovers March 1958

Billy Liddell and Liverpool 1960/61 squad

'Liddellpool' flag on the Kop at Anfield, October 2020

unplayable and the leather ball soaked, subsequently turning it into the proverbial medicine ball (as it was often called). Billy was tracking his man back and used his head to block a cross, but he was emphatically floored and concussed. Nevertheless, after the 'magic sponge' treatment from trainer Albert Shelley, he was deemed fit to play on, donning a large head bandage. It was commented how unsteady Billy became on a boggy pitch, then a further stoppage occurred after his bandage came loose from another headed clearance. Paisley too was later floored by heading the incomprehensibly heavy and dangerous ball.

The decision to continue playing may have had unknown long-term health issues for Billy but worked well for Liverpool on the day. He assisted their opener, with stand-in captain Jack Balmer emphatically finding the back of the net. Before half-time and despite a Sunderland equaliser, Billy was credited with the goal that came directly from a corner. His delivery from corners resulted in several direct goals during his career, although it does appear that at least some could have been accredited as own goals from the chaos caused by his wicked delivery. Liverpool won 4-1 and were now firmly in the race for the title. Billy Liddell was of pivotal importance.

Liverpool managed to juggle an intense title race with a cup run. Billy scored in their first match, a 5-2 third round victory away to Walsall. The cup run then saw them beat Grimsby, Derby and Birmingham before facing Burnley in the semi-finals. The quality of George Kay's men was obvious and their league form was transmitted to the FA Cup, while they were out for revenge after Burnley's 1914 FA Cup Final victory over Liverpool.

The match finished 0-0 after 90 minutes and extra time, taking them to a replay in mid-April. Over 50,000 supporters crammed into Man City's Maine Road, where George Kay was confident of a strong performance and a trip to Wembley. The first match's stalemate dragged on and on, Billy later commenting that he was convinced the match would enter a third instalment, but it was not to be. Fifteen minutes from the end, Burnley scored from a corner and Liverpool could not recover before being dumped out of the FA Cup.

Much was made of Liverpool's 'extreme wingers' in the *Daily Post* following the match. This again ties into the previous point of Billy not being fully utilised yet; he was there to serve but not score. This was a crushingly disappointing failure to score in two attempts against Burnley, a team that was in the Second Division at the time. A painful lesson, but perhaps one that served the club well for the immediate title run-in and the attacking philosophies of future seasons.

* * *

Bouncebackability is a phrase made popular by Iain Dowie and his Crystal Palace side from 2003/04. Liverpool in April

1947 had lost their FA Cup semi-final and sat fifth in the league with seven matches remaining, but the fans were in for a dramatic close and an emphatic example of team spirit, fitness and ability.

The seven-match run-in began with one of their two remaining home matches that season. Sunderland at home saw Stubbins return to scoring ways. The board did have to address crowd behaviour in the following programme after the jeering of skipper Jack Balmer, who struggled to play through injury. The one goal was enough, however, to see a win secured.

Next, eighth-placed Aston Villa hosted the Reds not long after the news of Billy's selection for a combined Great Britain side. They were to face the Rest of Europe in a game billed as 'The Match of the Century'. Billy's first competitive season had impressed the whole British Isles and buoyed his Liverpool team-mates ahead of the Villa match. Despite going behind inside five minutes, the bold decision to hand Prescot-born inside-left Billy Watkinson his first appearance paid off as he scored a huge headed goal. Then quick thinking by the club captain Willie Fagan following a Liddell free kick saw Liverpool go 2-1 up before half-time and they hung on to win again.

Busby's Anfield return should have been an exhibition match in appreciation of his services, but instead it was a match between his second-placed United and a fifth-placed but climbing George Kay Liverpool team. Hopes were low of achieving anything more than a fourth-placed finish, but the players played with the desire that they were ready to compete for every point, just in case. Liverpool had to win to keep any hopes alive in this their final Anfield match of the season, and in the 12th minute Billy carried the ball past Johnny Carey before sucking in the rest of the United defence and keeper as he entered the box. He pulled the ball back to Stubbins, who scored at a third attempt, following a goal line scramble. Kay's relentless Reds rolled on with another win.

Now fourth and three points behind Wolves, the final four matches were becoming increasingly more important. Billy's Great Britain escapade meant he missed Liverpool's next match on a day when Everton were facing table-topping Wolves and the red side of Merseyside was praying for a favour. Liverpool's opponents Charlton had just beaten Burnley in the FA Cup Final but were without the presence of their captain (and future Liverpool manager) Don Welsh, who was injured for the match. The subsequent Stubbins hat-trick in London may have had Liverpool thinking what could have been if they had defeated Burnley. There was enough to distract the Anfield faithful, though; a 3-1 victory for them and a surprise 3-2 win by Everton made a dream ebb ever closer.

The still Liddell-less Liverpool next played Brentford, Bob Priday filling in for Billy against the already relegated Bees, who were bolstered by the return of their Great British representative right-half Archie Macaulay. Despite the gulf in supposed quality and importance of the match, it was not an easy game. This mammoth season was now in mid-May and 40 league matches deep, Paisley was badly hurt from a tackle and had to leave the pitch for a side that was already without Liddell (Great Britain) and Taylor (England), and the winning run came to an end. Despite Priday scoring an undeserved goal late on, Brentford equalised through George Stewart with just over five minutes left. Remarkably, results continued to fall in favour with Red dreams as they dodged a bullet, making them happy with a point.

The penultimate match of the season was at Highbury against Arsenal. Liverpool were struggling, as Taylor was still away with England, Paisley was out of the final two matches and Billy had been injured playing for Great Britain. This was only helped by Arsenal having nothing to play for. George Kay's squad was being tested to the maximum as he patched up his side for a monumental match. Wolves, United, Stoke and Liverpool were all separated by one point with one further match to go. George Kay was not present as he was 'on business' (one can only imagine what could be so important) so Willie Fagan and Jack Balmer led their side into the match. Disaster struck on the hour mark as Arsenal's Ian MacPherson scored, leaving the men adorned in white with a bigger task on their hands.

The influential Scouser, Jack Balmer, so often deputising for Fagan as captain amidst the Scot's transfer speculation, clawed his team back into the match. His powerful header from a corner delivered by the Villa hero Watkinson, in just his fifth match, gave them hope. Balmer was again influential as he latched on to a Priday shot-come-cross, which deflected off an Arsenal defender, Walley Barnes, and found its way into the goal to secure a 2-1 triumph.

Twelve months after the North American trip, on Saturday, 31 May 1947, the Reds met fellow title-chasers Wolverhampton Wanderers in their last fixture of the season. The depth of Liverpool's squad was as surprising as it was significant, and Billy had thankfully been patched up in time to play. Liverpool had to win and then hope that Stoke, who would have to wait a further two weeks (mid-June!) to play their final match, failed to win at Sheffield United by enough goals to better Liverpool's goal average.

Wolves had a huge points advantage just weeks earlier but, as the *Liverpool Evening Express* hailed, it was 'a triumph of teamwork, consistency and individual ability … it was a storming finish with 11 out of the last 12 points won despite the fact that the last four matches were away from home'. Liverpool had put themselves in a position where they could make history.

Billy McConnell, the mastermind behind the trip to North America, had fallen ill before the match. He discharged himself from hospital pre-match as he knew it was a match for the ages. The boyhood Liverpool man who made his money from dockside cafes, was pivotal in selecting and tinkering with the side towards the end of the campaign. He was also instrumental in financing Liddell's and Stubbins's arrivals and the new club houses. Although well enough to attend the match, it was his final one as his illness sadly killed him in the following summer. The tragic suddenness of his death may have been eased by the fact that he was able to witness the final act of this theatrical campaign.

Encouraged by a returning Liddell and the absence of Wolves's ace marksman Denis Westcott, the match kicked off. Over 50,000 attended on a remarkably hot day, which was also to be Wolves skipper Cullis's final match of his career. It was clear that Liverpool were out to win, and quickly. First came the increasingly influential Balmer's goal in a move orchestrated by Billy, who started the match at outside-right. He and Priday linked up before Balmer calmly put Liverpool ahead on 20 minutes. The Wolves onslaught began but they were kept at bay before a sucker punch second by Stubbins, who put the ball past the Wolves keeper after breaking from a corner at pace.

It remained like that going into half-time – they just had to hang on. Wolves scored from a corner 20 minutes into the second half and nerves were jangling but Liverpool held on. Post-match celebrations saw Balmer carried on his team-mates' shoulders, just six matches after being jeered by his supporters. The agonising two-week wait now began.

The season was already being coined the greatest in Liverpool's 55-year history. Stoke were now to play the match of their lives, searching for a trophy they had never won and have never won since. Sheffield United's 38-year-old inside-left Jack Pickering was given his first competitive match for eight years and scored inside three minutes. Stoke drew one back before Pickering scored again on the stroke of half-time.

Liverpool supporters were following the match at Anfield due to the Liverpool Senior Cup Final against Everton being played on the same day at the same time. The Anfield scoreboard displayed the Stoke scoreline, and when it changed to 2-1 it was pandemonium in the stadium. Liverpool were winning 2-1 at Anfield and on the cusp of a Lancashire Cup, Liverpool Senior Cup and league title treble, two of them in the same hour. All eyes were pinned on the scoreboard, not the Merseyside derby.

Five minutes before the end of the Anfield action, the tannoy announcement confirmed Sheffield United's victory. Hats were flung in celebration and for the first time since the 'Untouchables' back-to-back title-winning side of the early 1920s, Liverpool were champions. Twenty-four years of hurt, wartime, depression, slums and bombings culminated in the most dramatic title race and unexpected victory.

Billy was more than involved, playing 40 matches in his 'first' season with Liverpool and gaining a league winners' medal to boot. He was of phenomenal importance and had he not been playing and injured for Great Britain, he would have played in the entire league run-in. The most unbelievable footballing season rolled into his trip to North America, and his marriage to Phyllis, all in the same year that war had ended and being given his first home by the club. As years and seasons go, Billy had all but peaked at the very start.

It is quite sad that Billy's medal collection stopped with the 1946/47 league title, but it is also fair to assume that little could ever top *that* campaign. As Billy's stature and ability grew, Liverpool's declined, and the loss of McConnell was a huge part of this. When Shankly arrived 12 years later, his constant battles with the board showed the decline after this season. Had McConnell, Kay and Liddell remained together, who knows the riches the club could have seen.

The Men Who Put the Pool into Liddellpool – Alan Banks

Alan Banks – Liverpool FC (1956–1961)

I was born 200 yards behind the Kop and I've been a Liverpool fan all of my life. Bill was my idol. In saying that, he was the idol of everybody. He was that sort of person; he was a truly great player.

Bill was a bit quiet, but he did like a laugh and a joke. He more or less kept himself to himself, but he was a lovely, lovely man. He was Liverpool, they didn't call them 'Liddellpool' for nothing. Billy carried the club for so many years, he was an unbelievable player for the club.

I made my full debut for Liverpool in September 1958, we played Brighton and had about 34,000 fans. Bill wasn't fit to play in that game, but he played in the following home game against Sheffield United and the crowd then was 44,000 people. That's the impact he had on the supporters at Liverpool, Bill. He would speak to all the young lads. My very first game that I played with Bill for the first team was against Sheffield United and I sat next to him. Bill was playing centre-forward in those days and I was playing inside-forward. He just said, 'Go out and play your natural game and enjoy it.'

I was very nervous. I'm sitting next door to my idol. For me, it was the highlight of my whole career. I played for 20 years but playing and sitting next to Bill was absolutely incredible.

I couldn't go any higher than having Billy sitting next to me. Bill had two great feet, he was fast, he was strong, and he was a great header of the ball as well. I pity some of the full-backs he used to play against when he was in his prime.

I don't know whether many people realise but Bill was only a part-time player. He only trained on a Thursday and Tuesday morning and then he went off to work. We only saw him on those two mornings and on a Saturday when he was playing.

He was a real gentleman on and off the field and he was absolutely idolised by the supporters. He was one of the greatest players ever to play for the club. I would put him alongside Kenny Dalglish and Steven Gerrard as the three greatest players ever to play for Liverpool. That's how I rate Billy. We've had so many great players down the years, but Bill is one of the best you'd ever see.

When I was a young kid, I used to stand on the Boys' Pen, which was right in the corner of the Kop. Those days, Bill was playing outside-left and when the ball went out to

Billy on the left wing, the crowd used to go 'woah', used to go mad because Bill was on the ball.

The feeling was exactly the same whether I was playing in the reserves or the first team with him. It was a life's ambition really. To see him play, all the years I had watched him and then now to be playing alongside him, it was fantastic. It was just nice to know that I knew Bill and that I played with him. I wasn't the only one, there were a lot of young kids in the reserves who looked up to Bill. We were just grateful to have a chance to play with him and watch him play.

One game I do remember, Liverpool had just got relegated in 1954 and Everton got promoted. Everton were the bigger club and we were picked to play against them in the third round of the FA Cup in 1955. In that time, Liverpool hadn't won an away game and Everton were riding high in the First Division. The game was at Goodison Park and it was a 75,000 all-ticket game. Liverpool finished up winning 4-0. Laurie Hughes was the centre-half and got injured. They moved Laurie Hughes on to the left wing and put Billy at centre-half. I tell you what, he was man of the match at centre-half. Bill would have been outside-left and, because there were no substitutes in those days, they shoved Laurie Hughes on the left wing and put Billy centre-half. He scored in that game as well.

He carried Liverpool for so many years, it was incredible. I don't know who the hell thought of calling it 'Liddellpool' but whoever thought of it deserves a medal! For myself, being a Scouser, to play for Liverpool and to play with my idol, not only my idol but the idol of everyone, it was just a pure pleasure.

5

FA Cup Final 1950

Well, here we are. On the way to Wembley on the day, and what a day. The prospect was indeed a wet one, really very bad luck on the tens of thousands crowding in to enjoy the tremendous thrills of a cup final. Quite a number out of the vast travelling football fans have come by car, regardless of expense. But, as a matter of fact, neither the price of petrol nor the filthy weather could stop anyone's enjoyment on this afternoon.

Then forth came the teams, Arsenal in yellow shirts and white shorts, Liverpool in white shirts and black shorts. His Majesty the King came out to meet them, first the Arsenal men were presented by their captain Joe Mercer. Then, Liverpool by their skipper Phil Taylor. Taylor won the toss from Mercer and a few seconds later, the rivals were all set to go …

LIFE WAS good, and the dawn of the 1949/50 season, well before the words from Movietone quoted opposite were to be heard, began with some fantastic Liddell family news. Billy's younger brother, Tom, was signed by Liverpool from Lochore Welfare in June 1949 after showing potential in his junior football, also with Lochgelly Violet. He was signed as a promising young full-back to add depth to the squad. The 12 stone, 5ft 10in younger brother of Billy joined Liverpool at 25. As has been mentioned, he did not play for the first team, but it was great for all the family to have two brothers in the same squad.

The Reds entered the season off the back of a mediocre previous campaign, where they had finished 12th with an unwanted yet impressive statistic. They had won the fewest number of home matches in the league, just five in 21 attempts but still managed to maintain impressive crowds, averaging over 44,000 for the season. The club was certainly indebted to their loyal supporters and needed to ensure they brought some joy this time around.

Billy had been a key figure again, playing 42 of a possible 52 matches, but his tally of nine goals would prove to be the fewest he would record in all but one campaign before his retirement season. Testament to his role that year though, Billy came second in Sportsman of the Year for 1949, behind 1948 Olympic double silver and World Championship gold medallist, cyclist Reg Harris. Billy was ready to be unleashed on the new season, which was to be the one where he played the most matches of his whole career.

The Liddell brothers began the pre-season in ordinary footballing form. July is, and always will be, a dreaded month of fitness for footballers. Returning to match fitness meant losing weight and gaining muscle ahead of an August curtain raiser for the new season. Liverpool would report to Anfield at 10am on the first pre-season morning to be weighed by trainer Albert Shelley. They would then don their training equipment, described by Albert Stubbins as 'sweaters and football knickers, over which are worn flannel trousers, and complete with a heavy pair of shoes'.

Equipped in their training gear, they would then begin a five-mile walk-come-jog in the July sun. This would be repeated daily, two sessions in the morning and afternoons of running, sprints and gym exercise to prepare them for a gruelling season ahead. Billy was, of course, still part-time; he would train full-time during July and then only Tuesdays and Thursdays throughout the campaign, while maintaining his accountancy job. The club trusted that he could juggle his accountancy and fitness, something that he never let the team down with.

There was more reason for this to be another milestone Liddell season, as Phyllis gave birth to twin boys Malcolm and David in March 1950. The first grandchildren of James and Montgomery were welcomed with another family visit from the Townhill Liddells.

As Tom, Malcolm and David all arrived in Liverpool during the 1949/50 campaign, it was to be George Kay's last full season with the Reds. His importance to Billy and Liverpool was prodigious. The Manchester-born right-half had captained the West Ham side in the first-ever Wembley FA Cup Final in 1923, where they were defeated 2-0 by his former side, Bolton Wanderers. The match became known as 'The White Horse Final' due to Billie the horse having to enter the field of play as 10,000 surplus supporters spilled on to the pitch due to overcrowding.

Kay also fought with the British Army during the First World War, which served as a four-year interruption to his football career. He fell ill during a tour of Spain, which caused him to retire from football while in his mid-thirties in 1926, after over 200 West Ham appearances.

His managerial break came at Luton Town, where he spent two seasons before moving to Southampton. The Second Division side languished in mid-table throughout Kay's tenure in the early 1930s; however, the club's poor financial state meant that the best players were readily sold to the highest bidder, disrupting Kay's plans. Finances got so bad that the whole board of directors resigned and Kay was advised to follow their lead.

George Patterson had fallen ill during his second spell as Liverpool manager, and the opportunity to replace him with the experienced, respected and unfortunate George Kay was snapped up by the Liverpool directors. Testament to his character, Kay remained at Southampton unpaid to see out the final few matches of his last season.

Kay arrived at Anfield during the same calendar year as Billy. Managers in this era were more trainers than team selectors and Kay, alongside Albert Shelley, whom he brought with him from Southampton, revolutionised the fitness of the Reds. War again interrupted Kay's plans and he was tasked with attempting to field a team each week during the war without being handed the opportunity to get to know many of his players before war broke out.

His networking and personable attitude made him popular amongst many players and he managed to gain their trust and dedication to repeatedly turn out for Liverpool during the war. Bill McConnell's decision to travel to North America in 1946 was readily supported by Kay, illustrating his ability to share responsibility and big decisions and his adeptness at promoting fitness and nutritional importance to football sides.

Kay was well read in psychology and philosophy and, while being quietly spoken, knew how to get the best out of his players, no better example being the dramatic 1946/47 title win. The rigmarole of handling a side now expected to repeat their league title feat weighed heavily on Kay, and by 1950 illness had taken a huge toll on him mentally and physically. Despite the board trusting him so much that they extended his contract by five years in the summer of 1950, he retired through ill health in January 1951.

Kay's ability to captain West Ham through the end of the First World War and manage Liverpool after the ensuing conflict, illustrates the strength of character and leadership he had. The players loved working under him and he delivered the only piece of silverware that Billy achieved. If he had not been so personable to James and Montgomery in 1938, the Billy Liddell story certainly would have been set away from Merseyside.

Although the players were not yet to know, they were to deliver one of the biggest days in Liverpool history and George Kay's career in this very season. This FA Cup campaign was to be the most significant at Anfield for nearly 40 years and would only later be topped by Ian St John's Wembley heroics in 1965.

Billy was pivotal on the route to Wembley, playing in all seven FA Cup matches and all at outside-left. First up was a rather drab affair, a 0-0 draw at Ewood Park against Blackburn Rovers. Surprisingly, more fans travelled to this tie than did for the 1947 Burnley semi-final at the same ground. The draw meant that Second Division Blackburn would have to come to Anfield for a replay. Billy was fundamental in dragging the Reds across the line, his link-up play with Paisley being a key part of the eventual victory. Billy's free kick that thundered off the bar was also mightily unlucky. Coming from behind, Liverpool went on to win 2-1 and the winner came as a result of another troublesome Liddell set piece.

The fourth-round tie set up the arrival of Third Division Exeter City. Their centre-half Ray Goddard made his first return to Anfield since Billy's debut in the 7-4 victory over Chelsea. The scoreline was better for Goddard but not what he would have wanted. The late January Merseyside rain played havoc with the playing surface, causing a soggy affair in which Billy's pace worked against him, as his feet could not get going in the thick mud. Goals from Kevin Baron, Willie Fagan and Jimmy Payne saw Liverpool through to face Stockport County.

More Third Division opposition meant Liverpool were again favourites to progress to the quarter-finals, something they had only done twice before in their history. Stockport supporters flocked to Edgeley Park in their droves, so much so that a fence collapsed during the match, causing supporters to tumble on to the pitch. The plan to mark Billy out of the game was a mark of respect, and each time he received the ball he was closely followed and swiftly scythed. Yet the opening goal came through some Liddell wing wizardry as his cross was knocked down by Paisley and Willie Fagan finished off the attack. Stubbins made it two before a fruitless consolation Stockport goal ended the match 2-1.

Three days following the birth of his twins, Billy welcomed Liverpool's first FA Cup First Division opposition in Blackpool. His opening match as a father was marked by hordes of Blackpool fans travelling in fancy dress to watch their Stanley Matthews-less side, the same team who went on to reach three FA Cup finals in six seasons from 1947. Accompanied by a dyed yellow duck and its own pail of water, the tangerine travelling supporters were out for a party. The away support was dampened when a Liddell corner caused chaos before Willie Fagan put the ball in the back of the net. Laurie Hughes's handball allowed Blackpool back into the tie from the penalty spot, causing Kay to switch Liddell and Jimmy Payne in hope of securing a win without a replay.

The two, now on different wings, linked up superbly as Payne set Billy up on the edge of the box. He expertly curled the ball into the top-right corner and sent the crowd into delirium. There was a nervy concluding ten minutes before the final whistle relieved the tension. The news over the tannoy that Everton had also progressed to the semi-final was met with cheers as the prospect of an all-Merseyside final loomed, but it was to be red vs blue in the semi-finals instead.

Merseyside travelled to Manchester and Liverpool returned to the scene of their 1947 FA Cup semi-final heartache at Maine Road. They were also out for revenge following the only previous semi-final clash between the sides, the 1906 2-0 defeat in a season where Everton went on to win their first FA Cup. This match being played on the same day as the Grand National meant it was a festival day for Merseyside sport.

Liverpool went into the match as favourites, with their potent attack and Billy ensured he would be at Wembley for the final. Prior to the match, he and Everton defender

Jackie Grant made a pact that whoever lost would give the other six tickets to the Wembley final. The opening goal came through Jimmy Payne's wing play. His cross found its way to Paisley, who lofted the ball back towards goal. Billy jumped with the Toffees keeper George Burnett, causing him to lose flight of the ball, and Paisley's effort looped into the goal. Over 70,000 supporters were in attendance and the Red contingent went ballistic in jubilation as Liverpool were 1-0 up at half-time.

The second half saw Billy score one of his most iconic Liverpool goals, turning Eddie Wainwright inside out and causing him to inadvertently keep the ball in play instead of conceding a corner. Billy took the ball past him and into the box before an emphatic finish that all but secured a passageway to Wembley. Billy continued to disturb the Everton defence, footage of him barging Burnett testament to the era of football. Several clear seconds pass from the Everton keeper catching the ball and Liddell charging in, the mild-mannered Billy illustrating the strength needed to play in the *now* 1950s football.

Liverpool lived up to pre-match predictions and the final whistle was greeted with an explosion of excitement. The Reds were off to Wembley for the first time, to face Arsenal. They could enter the spectacle confident of beating the North Londoners. That same season they had already overcome them 2-1 at Highbury and 2-0 at Anfield, where a Liddell goal helped claim victory.

The first Wembley visit in Liverpool's second FA Cup Final was because the Crystal Palace stadium had hosted the 1914 final, as it had done for every year since 1895, with 1914 being the last occurrence. Interest was so high that over 100,000 Liverpool supporters applied for final tickets, queuing through the night in the hope of securing their entry to the national stadium for the first time ahead of a nervous wait to see whether they were successful in a ballot.

* * *

Billy's personal life and professional life had coincided so well in 1947 that it looked set to happen again, as the same year his twins were born and brother signed for Liverpool he was to play at Wembley. This was a day that was always looked back upon with pride by Billy. He was a firm Anfield favourite already and had now spent 12 years with Liverpool. His loyalty was both respected and acknowledged by the fans, who saw him as a key part of their dangerous attack.

The pre-match excitement and build-up was soured with news of Bob Paisley's possible omission from the starting line-up. Kay had reportedly instructed Paisley to remain defensive during the semi-final derby, but Paisley scoring the first goal illustrated his attention to Kay's words. This was partnered with Paisley being injured for four matches preceding the final, with Liverpool failing to win any of the four. However, Bob had informed Kay that he was fully fit to play against the Gunners and was hopeful of a return to the team.

The tail end of the season was disastrous for Liverpool. They had been unbeaten for the first 20 matches of the season and in early April sat top of the league with eight league matches and the FA Cup Final to play. A turn of fortune in a direct juxtaposition from 1947 saw the Reds slip so severely that they finished eighth, five points from the top. The 31-year-old Paisley discovered in the local press that he was out of the final following a vote amongst the directors. Supporters were devastated, as was Paisley, who seriously considered quitting Anfield that summer. Kay and the directors nearly had the blood of the 20 missing future honours that Paisley went on to win as manager on their hands.

There were nine directors and the vote was five to four in favour of Bill Jones starting the final. Rumours started to spread that Bill Jones's daughter was engaged to one of the directors but no evidence has been found to support this. However, it highlights the scandalous nature of this public decision to the loyal Reds supporters. Some fans even refused to go to watch Liverpool ever again in protest at the decision. The future quarrels between Shankly and members of the board, including T.V. Williams who was a member in 1950, highlight the nature of some of these businessmen in influential footballing positions.

Despite this, though, the supporters were so excited for one of the biggest matches in the history of the club, only their second cup final. Perhaps this is best illustrated by the song that was sung by the fans in the lead-up to the big day, to the tune of Teresa Brewer's '(Put Another Nickel In) Music, Music, Music':

Put another record on, Liverpool two and
Everton none.
All we want is a cup final ticket to Wembley,
Wembley, Wembley.
Albert scoring goals galore.
Billy Liddell scoring more.
All we want is a cup final ticket to Wembley,
Wembley, Wembley.
When we all go to Wembley,
You'll find the Everton team turning green, with
envy that cannot be seen.
So give three cheers for the good old reds.
They made the blues forget their heads.
We will bring the cup home soon from Wembley,
Wembley, Wembley.

Those lucky enough to be successful in the ticket lottery travelled by car and train for their first glimpse of the twin towers through steamed-up windows on a rainy April afternoon. Phil Taylor had the pleasure of leading the Reds out at Wembley, alongside the man whose shoes he would one day fill, George Kay. Taylor then introduced King George VI to his team-mates wearing white. This was after the Arsenal skipper had introduced him to the yellow shirt-adorning Gunners. This was the Ellesmere Port-born Joe Mercer, who had signed for Arsenal from Everton in 1946. He still lived in Liverpool and trained with the Reds weekly before travelling to Arsenal for matches, so that he could juggle his local greengrocer's business and London-based football.

It was to be a day of frustration and pain for Billy. Much as Stockport had attempted earlier in the competition, Arsenal highlighted him as the danger man and wanted to keep him quiet. His Scotland room-mate, right-half Alex Forbes, was tasked with marking Billy out of the game. Forbes, who was a member of the Sheffield United team that beat Stoke to hand Liverpool the title in 1947, performed a hatchet job on Billy for 90 solid minutes. Anytime Billy was within a sniff of the ball, Forbes quickly followed to hack him to the ground.

Billy had been so influential on the road to the final, which now finally kicked off, following Taylor winning the toss. This had little effect on proceedings as a terrific pass found Reg Lewis through on goal inside 20 minutes, and Arsenal were ahead. Shock was shared amongst the supporters due to Liverpool being the favourites, despite the disastrous season's end, as they had beaten Arsenal home and away during the season.

Billy found some rare freedom on the left wing soon after, his cross narrowly missing the head of Stubbins and rolling agonisingly past the striker. The start of the second half saw Billy again get the better of Forbes, Arsenal keeper George Swindin fumbling the resulting cross to the head of Stubbins, who again failed to convert. Arsenal remained ahead and Stubbins and Liverpool were to rue these missed chances.

Just following the hour mark, some clever midfield play again meant the ball found its way to Reg Lewis in the box, who scored his second goal for Arsenal. Billy had hoped the birth of his twins would provide luck on the day, but by a strange twist of fate, Lewis too had fathered twins that same year and the luck was more in his favour. Despite more Liddell-inspired waves of heroic attacks, Lewis's goals were enough for the win and to crush the Merseyside men on their big day. The terrible end to the season form, dropping Paisley and Kay's ill health all combined to ensure that it was not to be the day so many had hoped it would. Paisley, despite the disappointment, joined his team-mates on the pitch following the match to salute the travelling fans.

This was, of course, in the heyday of FA Cup importance, with no League Cup or European trophies available for Liverpool or anyone else to fight for, making this all the more painful. Billy had more than done his share of the work, as all the bright attacks were through him, despite his rough handling from Forbes. Phyllis Liddell, who had left the twins with childminders on Merseyside, was asked to help Billy change after the match due to the condition he had been kicked into.

Billy recalled: 'Alec did come in a bit high, with his boot raised, and he caught me down my arm and side with his studs, but it was nothing serious.' Remaining selfless and magnanimous in defeat, Billy was eager to deflect his upset and wanted to praise Arsenal. It was reported in the press that Liddell and Forbes would no longer room for Scotland, but Billy remained professional and never held anything against him. Despite obvious disappointment and being the match that Billy would change the result of if he could change only one from his career, there was still huge personal pride in being part of such an occasion.

This pride was echoed by the fans when the Liverpool players returned from Wembley. They were greeted by thousands of supporters to salute the team's effort. Police had to hold back the crowds from the open-top bus as they celebrated the labours of their heroes. Liddell and Stubbins, being fan favourites, gathered most of the attention, Stubbins holding a teddy bear thrown to him by an adoring fan. They were greeted by those lucky enough to be in attendance at Wembley, as well as the fans at home who had listened on the wireless, some on their acid bottle accumulator radios, others watching on television. The players then stood on the balcony of Liverpool Town Hall to thank the fans for their support on a huge day of pride for the club, regardless of the loss.

Despite his brutal kicking, Billy wanted to honour the loyal supporters and turn out for the final league match of the season at Anfield. His goal in another defeat was of personal significance, his 20th of the campaign making him the highest-scoring winger in all four English divisions. The disappointing end of the season was about to roll into a devastating blow to the Liddell family in January 1951.

The Men Who Put the Pool into Liddellpool – Johnny Morrissey

Johnny Morrissey – Liverpool FC (1955–1962)

I was a Red as a kid and I was a left-winger because of Billy Liddell. My father used to take me to the football and as I got older I used to go to the Boys' Pen, it was 'Liddellpool' then because he sat so prominent within the team and as a young kid I used to admire him.

He just seemed to be scoring every week; you could say he was my idol.

The first time I met him was when I signed for Liverpool. I was about 15 and I used to be dying to get in the dressing room to see him, but he was quiet, a bit introverted. In football a lot of banter goes on and mickey-taking in the dressing room, but he was never part of that. He was a quiet man and, to say he was such a big figure on the field, off the field he wasn't forward in any way at all. I was overawed but after a few weeks the strange becomes the norm and I was used to watching him getting his kit and his boots out and training with him.

Players like Laurie Hughes were very outspoken, and Ray Lambert was a mickey-taker, but Billy was never part of that, he was part of the dressing room but didn't get involved in the mickey-taking. It was unbelievable to be honest, if the public even knew what was going on, it was unbelievable. He sat quite central in the changing room and he did speak but he wasn't outlandish like some of them, but it was a dream world for me, to be honest.

I remember I couldn't get in the team on the left wing while Billy was playing and Alan A'Court played for England, so my chances got limited, but we were playing against Sunderland one year and I was about 18. Alan A'Court was on the right and he was on the edge of the penalty area on the wing and I remember him dragging the ball back like a right-winger does with his left foot, and he's hit this ball over and I'm looking at it. It was a bit too high so I'm thinking I will chest it because it was a bit too high and I shouted, 'My ball!' and I was just about to get it. Then, Billy Liddell, I don't know where he came from, and I can still see the bulge in his neck. He headed this ball and, honest to God, I couldn't have hit it harder with my foot. It bulleted into the net. It was amazing, at Sunderland's Roker Park, and I can remember that to this day.

He was strong and pacey with it; anybody tackling him would be brushed off, the man was that strong. He didn't have a tremendous physique and must have been about 5ft 10in. I think it was just all solid muscle. When I think back, he made so many runs from the halfway line, Bob Paisley would just give him the ball. I can remember all the times I watched him as a kid running from the halfway line and the power and the strength of him, it was incredible. He would be great in the modern game, left- and right-footed as well.

The fans loved him, the Anfield roar now was the same then. You would get goose pimples when you were playing. They would cheer the team, but although there was no chanting or anything then, there was a roar when he got the ball.

Bill Shankly was a big admirer of Billy Liddell. He would have been in awe of Billy and he wasn't in awe of many, Shanks, but he was in awe of Billy Liddell. He was past it when Shanks got there but for the man he was and for what he had done for Liverpool, Shanks admired him.

As a player, he would give 110 per cent. He was a leader, other lads playing would draw strength from him and he was a good club man. He was a quiet man, didn't speak a lot. 'Liddellpool' was the right word for them because he was the main man. Liverpool have had so many good players after Billy but most of the players Liverpool had when he played were good or average but not great. You must bear in mind a lot of great players came after him, the likes of Emlyn Hughes and all these types of players. I would say he was the first great Liverpool player in my eyes, from what I can remember, definitely!

He was a fabulous player who gave a good 110 per cent, and 110 per cent of good ability. He was a very positive player, didn't dilly dally when he got it, and he would make a beeline for the goal or down the wing. Any accolades that were presented to him he deserved.

6

Life in Liverpool,
Outside of Football

IN JANUARY 1951, Montgomery penned a letter to Billy
and Phyllis updating them on her health:

> Mum [Montgomery speaking about herself] is on
> her feet but she feels her back by night, the doctor
> was in on Thursday and he prescribed a yellow
> pill which I have to put under my tongue and let
> it dissolve, and another pill which is blue. This
> contains a powder which I have to take (two) before
> returning to bed … Excuse the unusual scrawl, put
> it down to weakness. The doctor is calling in to see
> me some time again next week. Hope I feel stronger
> then. Well folks, must close now and get off back to
> bed again … Phyllis and Bill, we send our best love
> to you and may you see all the joys with your family
> as we did with ours.
>
> Mum and Dad, sister and brothers

Little did Billy know when Montgomery wrote this letter that just ten days later one of his parents would sadly die. As illustrated in this communication, Montgomery was not well and did note to Billy that she was 'glad to see you have steered clear of the epidemic yourselves'.

The 1951 influenza epidemic caused an unusually high death toll in England and in particular Liverpool, weekly deaths being higher than those of the 1918 pandemic. In 1918, the pandemic coined the Spanish flu infected around 500 million people worldwide. For this epidemic in 1951 to top those figures in Liverpool illustrates the severity of the issue. However, it was the Liverpool Liddells that would be travelling to visit their Townhill family due to illness that year.

The *Liverpool Echo* noted on 27 January ahead of the match away to Charlton: 'Both Willie Liddell and his brother Tom were recalled to Scotland, where their father is seriously ill, on Wednesday (24th). Liverpool half expected that Willie Liddell would be able to come down and play at Charlton but he could not, and so Cyril Done came in at outside-left.' The *People Report* corroborated with their comments: 'The man who really decided this game [Charlton 1-0 Liverpool] was an absentee – Billy Liddell. The left-winger had been called to Scotland at the last minute because of the illness of his father. Had he been present, Liverpool – I lay a Hulme shilling to a Seed cigar – would have won 4-1.'

It was clear that Liverpool were missing Billy on the pitch, but he and Tom had to travel north to see their father in hospital. Despite the influenza epidemic, James Liddell died on 29 January 1951 at 54 years old. The retired coal miner died at 10.05am from hypertension pneumoconiosis cardiac failure. Montgomery had noted in the past that James had not been well but he refused to visit a doctor.

Her letter to Billy is rather chilling as she is clearly fearful of her own health and that of Billy, Phyllis, Malcolm and David, but it was James who was in the most need of attention. His typical mid-20th-century manner of being too tough for hospital and medication killed him early. Obviously, his job in the mines was a huge factor in his early death but he died 14 years younger than his father William had, who was also a miner.

This macho projection of illness regarded as weakness is no doubt a key factor in Billy's attitude to head injury. You cannot blame James and Billy for this; it was a cultural issue at the time where men had to be men. Nevertheless, this must be highlighted today. Any illness, mental or physical, needs to be attended to correctly. James did not live to see the entirety of his son's phenomenal career and Billy's latter years were taken from him because of a terrible disease.

There has not been enough research or funding into the inextricable link between footballing head injuries, particularly those caused to players by the old-fashioned leather balls, and dementia, which includes Alzheimer's, vascular, frontotemporal and Lewy body dementias. All these diseases fall under the umbrella of dementia. It is important that head injuries in sport are much more closely assessed so that more people can spend more time with their sporting family members and enjoy their memories before they are taken away from them. During the BBC documentary *Dementia, Football and Me*, hosted by Alan Shearer, it was found that 'former professional footballers were three and a half times more likely to die of dementia' and that the balls were nearly twice as heavy when wet. These two facts illustrate how dangerous these balls were and playing football was during this era.

Without wanting to reveal the private health conditions of ex-players when writing this book, a stark statistic feels best placed here. Billy Liddell played with 93 different players during his time at Liverpool – only nine are alive today. Of those nine players, more than half of them are currently struggling and living with forms of dementia. Granted, these men are aged between 80 and 90, but for half of them to have the same disease is as upsetting as it is anger-inducing. If half the people in any workplace were diagnosed with the same illness there would be no doubt of a link – there is no difference with football.

As for James's death, this was from a profession that has all but died out in Britain today. The miners of this era were as important as they were brave. Dockers and miners were huge parts of Townhill and Liverpool during Billy's life and the industry it provided was great for the areas, particularly in their recovery from the war. The subsequent removal of these industries and the lack of support from the sycophantic Tory government headed by Maggie Thatcher left places like Merseyside and Dunfermline in ruin.

James's death is as strongly linked to mining as it is bravado. There are too many men afraid to admit they are ill and admit they are struggling. If the call for football governing bodies is to help with the battle with dementia, then the call to men to look after their health is as loud. Anyone too scared or who believes they are too strong or brave to admit they are ill needs to get themselves to the doctor. The cough could be a slight cold, it could be lung cancer. The heart pain could be acid reflux, or it could be hypertension pneumoconiosis cardiac failure and you could die at 54, missing your child become a legend in their sport and watching your grandchildren grow up. Your health is your biggest asset, so look after that and live a long and happy life with those who love you the most.

Montgomery was talking to Billy about how she felt, and the pills prescribed by the doctor may well have saved her life. Billy was a man in his twenties, and being the eldest male and most financially secure, he was now the man at the helm of the Liddell family and was about to display courage, leadership and compassion tenfold of what he had done on the Anfield pitch.

* * *

In October 1951, Billy moved his family down to Liverpool. Since Billy and Tom were able to spend time with their father before he died, James was able to make a request of his eldest son. He asked whether he would look after the family in his absence. Montgomery had little of her own family left in the area and James worried for her safety and ability to pay for the home and children. As Billy could not abandon Liverpool due to Phyllis's family, his twins, playing for Liverpool and his accountancy career lined up for retirement, the only option was Liverpool for the Liddell clan.

Billy put his family in the club house provided for him in 1947, on Westfield Avenue. He approached the club and asked whether he could purchase the property from them to house his family and then arranged his move to Windsor Road in Tuebrook, around five minutes from Anfield in the car. Billy, Phyllis, David and Malcolm moved to Windsor Road, while Montgomery, Campbell, Alastair, George, and Rena inhabited Westfield Avenue. The club was more than accommodating to help Billy during such a tough time.

The two houses were close to each other and Billy could comfortably look after his mum and younger siblings, knowing they were in a safe area around his team-mates. When they arrived in the October at Westfield Avenue, they were welcomed by birthday cards for Montgomery's 54th birthday. All the family in Scotland were keen to ensure she settled into her new home at what would have been a traumatic time.

Credit must also go to Phyllis, who was happy to aid her husband and give up her family home. Meanwhile, Billy shouldered the responsibility as a promise to his late father. The family did settle into their Liverpool abode and called Westfield Avenue home for the rest of Montgomery's life. Billy was fortunate to be able to financially support his family, although there is a large disparity between wages then and now. However, this house move does illustrate his relative wealth through football and accountancy.

Billy's money was perhaps more far-reaching than his time could be, so Tom was also tasked with helping the family settle in. Although forever in his brother's football shadow, Tom was only 20 months younger and played a big role in helping his family. Tom would be the practical help for Montgomery, Alastair, George and Rena and he would attend to any odd jobs, while keeping family morale high.

Montgomery had initially been apprehensive about Billy moving to Liverpool and now she had to face the same prospect herself. Although she was anxious, she had little choice about her own move. She did grow to love the city though, in the end, but she had to convince George and Rena that they were right to stay in Liverpool with her, as they had been upset at leaving their friends in Scotland.

Mrs Liddell soon found work in the Kardomah Café on Basnett Street, then she went to North John Street. Bizarrely, the lack of health and safety in ice cream production was the cause of her hand becoming crippled. As she was handling ice cream all day with no gloves or knowledge of any repercussions, her hand became undeterrably seized. This meant that Alastair soon had to head to work to help his mother pay the bills, working as a baker in St Helen's Bakery and then he worked in Ray's Bakery in Prescot, before getting his own shop.

Campbell came down with the family but he did not stay long. They had a family sweet shop but did not enjoy the lifestyle or the area. His wife did not like Liverpool and wanted to return home as her parents were still alive, so they went back. Billy, being the new head of the family, saw this as a defeat. He was trying to do well by his family, moving them all down to Merseyside and helping set them all up with housing and jobs. Campbell's leaving Liverpool did ruin the relationship between the brothers and the family, and moving Campbell's son with them meant that Montgomery lost access to her grandson as well.

One frequent visitor to the new Liddell residence was Tom Ogilvie, part of the Cowdenbeath-supporting side of the family. Billy's 11-year-old cousin would come and see the family soon after their move, marvelling at the opportunity to be in the same street as Eddie Spicer and Bob Paisley whenever he visited. Spotting his football obsession, Billy would take Ogilvie to training with George, and the two young boys would help as ball boys for the squad.

This again illustrates the pedigree of Billy; he was definitely provided special treatment by the club helping to move his family, signing his brother Tom and then allowing his cousin and brother to come to help in training. They certainly tried to repay the performances of Billy and his loyalty. Billy knew he would now be looked upon as a father figure to the younger members of his family and made a conscious effort to look after and treat them as best he could.

This time to reclaim his family bonds and living with them day in, day out really strengthened the ties between them. Some of their favourite pastimes were religion and Scottish dancing, and by 1951 Billy belonged to a Liverpool and District St Andrews Scottish Dancing Society. Montgomery was the first to partake alongside Billy and they would drive to and from dancing together. Billy loved Scottish dancing and he also always belonged to a church in Liverpool. He was one of the founder members of Court Hey Methodist Church in Huyton. He had always been a churchgoer, and upon his returns to Scotland would enjoy speaking in the church in Dunfermline, where his theme was 'Play Up and Play the Game'. He was a real Christian, and this was a passion of the whole family.

Billy's relationship with the Church meant that he also used to be a Sunday school teacher in Court Hey. To think that he was doing this while playing football is amazing and testament to his faith. Alongside his friend Alec, referred to

LIFE IN LIVERPOOL, OUTSIDE OF FOOTBALL

as the two stooges, he would love entertaining the children with his farcical comedy shows and pantomimes.

Billy's religion meant that he never played or trained on a Sunday. Much like with his namesake but no relation Eric Liddell, religion could interfere with sport. Eric was a Christian missionary and during the 1924 Paris Olympics the 100-metre heats were held on a Sunday. Although this was his best event, he refused to partake and was disqualified but then went on to win gold in the 400 metres. His life is depicted in the 1981 Oscar-winning film *Chariots of Fire*. Fellow Scot and Liddell, Billy was the same and would have abstained from football in line with his beliefs. Although much is made of his misfortune in the riches and medals he missed out on due to the era he played in, Billy is also lucky that football was never played on a Sunday during his career.

Another activity and pastime that Billy was involved in was his freemasonry. This stemmed from people he met in the Church and they would attend yearly visits to Llandudno. Liddell was initiated as a freemason in Liverpool Epworth Lodge in 1949. He was exalted also as a Royal Arch freemason in 1971. As per the Museum of Freemasonry:

Freemasonry is one of the oldest social and charitable organisations in the world. Its roots lie in the traditions of the medieval stonemasons who built our cathedrals and castles.

Organised freemasonry is over three hundred years old and began when, on 24 June 1717, freemasons from four London lodges met to form the world's first Grand Lodge. The United Grand Lodge of England (UGLE) is the governing body for freemasonry in England and Wales and is headquartered in Freemasons' Hall, London.

Freemasons use four important guiding principles to help define their path through life: Integrity, Friendship, Respect and Charity.

Membership is open to people from all backgrounds and the organisation's aim is to empower members to be the best they can be – it's about building character, supporting members as individuals and helping them make a positive contribution to society.

Freemasonry is also one of the largest charitable givers in the country, contributing over £48 million to deserving causes in 2018 alone. Freemasons don't only donate money, with over five million hours of volunteer work undertaken by freemasons in 2018.

The wider perception of freemasons is as an exclusive and secretive club, but Billy's presence demonstrates their charitable and morally righteous aims. He always kept this part of his life secret and solemn, as per the oath taken to become a freemason. He would attend Llandudno with about 20 to 30 others; they were all freemasons, and a few people from church joined him as the years passed. The yearly ritual was always excitably anticipated by all involved.

Becoming part of the Liddell family, after the fame of Billy, became a daunting prospect. That is if the person entering the family was aware of who he was! Betty Liddell entered that family through her marriage to George but never saw Billy as a celebrity or an imposing figure in the family. Betty was not a football fan and was only aware of Billy's status within the city after mentioning her new boyfriend's surname.

Speaking about Billy, Betty described him thus: 'He was just ever so quiet. He shook my hand and said pleased to meet you, but he was a very quiet man, his own person but he was lovely and he had a lovely family.' It was another issue getting to know what to call him. The family called him Bill, those in Scotland and who knew him in his very early Liverpool days called him Willie, but in Liverpool he became known as Billy on the pitch and in the media. Anyone calling him Bill is normally a good sign as to how well they really knew him.

The family would spend their evenings together several times throughout the week, Scottish dancing in Liverpool City Centre, near the Adelphi Hotel. On other nights they would go to the road made famous by the Beatles, Penny Lane, and partake in more Scottish dancing in a church hall. Montgomery, Billy, Tom, Alastair, George and Rena would all be regularly in attendance. Being proud Scots, the Liddell family was delighted to be able to continue their dancing within Liverpool. To become part of the Liddell clan, like Betty, it was imperative to be able to partake in the dancing, so the family grew ever larger.

Despite being so humble, Billy was able to take some advantage of his stardom. When he heard that George and Betty were going to see Frankie Vaughan live, he was quick to help make the event more special for them. Vaughan was a Liverpool-born singer and actor, coined 'Mr Moonlight' by his fans. Two of his most revered singles were 'The Garden of Eden' and 'Tower of Strength'. As Vaughan was involved in the same boys' clubs with Billy, Liddell managed to get himself, his wife, brother and sister-in-law backstage to see their hero during a gig on Sheil Road in Kensington, Liverpool.

Billy was a big advocate of boys' clubs and would volunteer a lot of his spare time to helping them raise money and attention. The purpose of the clubs was to keep young boys and girls in the city on the straight and narrow. He would often attend to give out awards and do talks alongside fellow 1960s Liverpool celebrities.

It was not just Frankie Vaughan, Eddie Braben was also a friend of Billy. Braben was another Liverpool-born celebrity, the comedy writer best known for his role of writing the material for comics such as David Frost, Ronnie Corbett, Ken Dodd and, most famously, Morecambe and

Wise. Braben, along with his wife Deidre, would always be amongst the Liddell family when they had gatherings. The presence of a comedy genius would mean there was always a lot of laughing. Billy's sister-in-law Betty always had the measure of Braben. She had a great sense of humour and this created some very happy times for the family.

Actress Anna Neagle was also involved in similar charity work to Billy but his most famous acquaintance was probably Ken Dodd, the Liverpool comedian. Billy would do a lot for Dodd in the comic's early days when Dodd was frequenting the working men's clubs. He did not have a car so Billy would drive him around, help with his props and generally support his friend's budding profession. The fact he was friends with comedians shows his enjoyment of it. Malcolm recalled how Billy loved watching slapstick comedy on TV and would laugh for hours. The juxtaposition of being the quiet, limelight-dodging man to being friends with some of the biggest stars in the city is stark. However, it is perhaps best described by David Liddell: 'I think it's because of who he was that people befriended him. He didn't go out seeking fame and fortune by being friends with others, that wasn't part of him.'

It is also unusual that Billy did not have many great footballing friends outside of football. Due to him being for much of his time at Anfield the only part-time player at the club, his absence meant that he was at a disadvantage in making the same kind of bonds that other players managed with each other. It has been said that his friend at Liverpool was Bob Paisley, so much so that Billy appeared on Bob Paisley's episode of *This is Your Life* in 1977. Despite this, the story he shared was one from inside the club:

> Just after the war, we had a commissionaire at Anfield by the name of Paddy Walsh. He used to always clean the manager's car and this particular day he had done a terrific job. It was really immaculate, the car, after what he had done and he was in the process of finishing the car off. He went to get a new bucket of water. Bob nipped in, opened the car doors and wound down the window. So, Paddy came along and not thinking threw the bucket of water right in through the car!

No doubt a great story and, of course, one example of many years of friendship. Billy and Bob lived opposite each other, would get the 61 bus to training and matches together and no doubt had a great deal of mutual respect. However, Billy left his football at Anfield, so his best friends were his family and those in the very inner circles of his life. He spent time with his fellow Westfield Avenue inhabitants Bob Paisley and Eddie Spicer, and their young families enjoyed growing up together.

With Billy being an abstainer from drinking and smoking, the players would play tricks on him. Billy enjoyed telling a tale of the players pouring alcohol in his orange juice, which he had to spit out. The fact he took it as comical shows how he could take a joke, but it also explains why he may not have wanted to spend much time with team-mates off the pitch.

This did not mean Billy had no time for others. Despite being so busy he would always be on hand to help, exemplified by the boys' clubs and the fact that he would do the books for the Scottish Dancing Society as well as any friends that would need help. He was the treasurer of one of the Sunday schools and he used to count the money out on his kitchen table at home. As thanks for his services, Billy was presented with a budgerigar. As kind as the gift was, the combination of a budgie and stacks of coins did not work too well. The bird would hop along the table before taking flight, so the piles of pennies would be fired around the room and Billy would have to start all over again. He loved being busy and was at his best with a hectic schedule, which is what kept him playing and working for so long.

All this was alongside Billy continuing to work with Simon Jude and West as an accountant. He would travel, auditing different businesses and continued his training to earn as many qualifications within accountancy as he could. His Liverpool team-mates would often comment on their jealously of Billy being able to lead another life off the pitch, something he was also fond of. He was clearly an intelligent man, the skills developed from his youth meaning he became a competent accountant and went on to enjoy the many newspaper articles he wrote religiously in later life. The fact he stayed devoted to the same team and accountancy firm that gave him a chance in 1938 is again testament to his loyalty.

Despite being a staunch Christian and passionate in his own beliefs of not swearing or drinking alcohol, Billy was a big fan of a party and a social gathering. He was a private family man, so it would only be close friends and family who were lucky enough to witness him in full flow. Being the non-drinker, with the biggest house, he was the perfect host. Lying on the ground and challenging his twin boys to lift him off the floor would have the family in hysterics as well as the many other games they enjoyed together. Drinks were always topped up and the taxi home was not needed due to Billy being sober and driving everyone back!

Although he did not enjoy seeing his sons, when they were of age, drinking in front of him, Billy did not frown upon others. He would revel in keeping glasses full and, as he had no personal experience of the taste, his measures would often be as deadly as one of his trademark cannon shots from his left foot.

Within the family, Montgomery and James were also teetotal and James encouraged his children to sign the pledge to not drink alcohol. Billy and Alastair did not drink, Tom very occasionally and Campbell only at Christmas and New Year. The age gap between the elder brothers and

Billy's twin siblings is perhaps best exemplified in their more liberal relationship with alcohol. In Rena's words, 'George and I made up for the rest!'

Montgomery would be in attendance for all gatherings and she used to play her harmonium in the 'posh' room, the entertaining room, of Billy's house. Billy's twins would help operate the pedals, one on hands and knees pushing the pedals down, while the other tried to play a tune. The joy of singing together as a family was obvious. James's favourite song was 'The Laughing Policeman', and they would always do a rendition in his honour.

Billy was different with his family – the star in the family but not the star of the family – illustrating how he was good at putting on a public face. He was still quiet and thoughtful but he would surprise those people welcomed into the family when he spoke, not just because it was out of character but because he was quite an eloquent speaker. Football was rarely the subject of conversation as Billy had a lot of other dealings with several other societies, such as the boys' clubs, etc. With football, he would answer when asked about it but felt as though people would look up to him as an ex-player but think he was being boastful discussing his own career.

The famous Scottish celebration of Hogmanay, celebrated on New Year's Eve, meant that Billy's house was the place to be for the wider Liddell family every year. He was the life and soul at those parties and loved a pun.

He would always make speeches at New Year, and would always be the head of the house. And it was a Scottish tradition that the head of the house wished everyone a Happy New Year.

Again, in stark contrast to his character as a restrained man, Billy would also be a showman in the privacy of his home and his church. He and Phyllis would star in pantomimes, where Billy played the ugly sister at Court Hey Church in 1951. The image of Billy dressed in slippers, a wig, flowery dress and an apron is as hilarious as it is seemingly astonishingly out of character. He also used to perform puppet shows for all the children with Tom during family events. There were several sides to Billy, and he was a showman on and off the pitch, more willingly at Anfield, however!

Despite his obvious and far-reaching fame in Liverpool, this was a different era of fandom. To put this into some context, the team of the generation was the England 1966 side. On the day of the final where they achieved glory and immortality, Bobby Charlton and Ray Wilson were free to peruse the aisles on a morning shopping trip. Players then were not less loved; they were just normal men with great footballing talent. Heroes and legends, yes, but the celebrity-chasing, selfie-hoarding fandom was not present. Billy would hear a chorus of 'hello, Mr Liddell', followed by the occasional request for his autograph or sporadic picture. Malcolm perhaps best described it, saying, 'When we used to go into Liverpool, we used to get stopped all the time when I was with my dad. As youngsters we just thought he had lots and lots of friends!'

Billy had time for every fan and loved to speak with supporters, whether during a run from Anfield to Melwood with Bill Jones or in the family shop owned by Tom and Billy on Walton Breck Road, in Walton near the stadium. One young supporter, Billy Howard, frequented the shop when he was a young teen and recalled moments of encouragement from Liddell: 'He told me that practice makes perfect and he signed my pictures. Some players would just walk past you, not so much in those days but certainly later, but Billy would always allow time for you.'

Billy's sons recalled the unusual yet ritualistic nature of his matchday breakfast of poached egg on toast and rice pudding. Billy would cook them the more palatable fried egg, bacon and porridge. His attention would then turn to the quick crossword in the *Daily Mail*. As his football days ended and his diet could become a bit less stringent, he was a huge fan of a Toblerone and, due to his drink abstinence, it became an easy Christmas and birthday present for the twins to buy!

The twins would often get the opportunity to travel to training and to matches at Anfield. They had a free roam of the stadium while their dad was receiving treatment in the physio room situated underneath the paddock. David recalled: 'Our father was in the treatment room under heat lamps and being treated with liniment. I always have this picture of Albert Shelley, who was his trainer, with a cigarette hanging out of his mouth.'

Billy's commitment to Liverpool, boys' clubs, accountancy, church, freemasonry, Scottish dancing, anything and everything else he got up to, did mean that he was away from the family home a lot. He took tremendous care of his physique and was a very driven character during his football and working life. David Liddell commented that 'really it was my mother who brought us up'.

In complete truth, those were the only words I heard during my research for this book that I believe Billy would be upset with. I am sure many contemporary footballers would feel some affinity with those words as they would be aware of the sacrifices that need to be made to be a professional footballer. Billy had an exceptionally long career due to his drive and commitment and it does appear that he may have toppled the work-life balance on some occasions. When the context of being a professional footballer who worked full-time is assessed though, it does make some sense that one part of his life would suffer.

David went on to say, 'My father was never really there because he was always playing football or was in some outlandish place. I never realised that when he played for Scotland, he would travel to lots of places. He had his other job as an accountant, so he was always quite busy with boys' clubs and that. He would often be away at night as he was a member of the Freemasons, so we didn't see a great deal of him really.'

Malcolm, in an attempt to share as much balance as possible, did also state, 'As a footballer, I get a lot of information about what he was like from people of a certain age who actually saw him play when he was at his peak. I couldn't say I knew a great deal about his football. But as a parent, he was the number one! He was a kind person who loved doing his daily crossword in the *Mail*. He was just a nice person.'

Billy's religious beliefs were not fully transferred to his sons. David remembered the stern response to him bringing beer into the family home in his twenties. Despite this disappointment, there were never arguments between the three males in the family. Billy wanted to pass on his beliefs but he was not someone to ram his religion or life choices down anyone's throat. The twins attended Sunday school in their youth and signed the abstainers' roll, not knowing what it really meant. When the temptations of later life revealed that they had agreed to give up alcohol, they quickly revoked their pledge.

When it came to swearing, Billy was as strict. Malcolm recalled a story of his father's disapproval to some dully coloured language:

David and I were taunting each other. I called him a stupid 'get' and my father said, 'Don't ever use that word again,' and at the time I didn't know what it meant and I found out eventually that it was the son of a prostitute. That was one instance where I saw him quite angry with us.

On another occasion, David and I shared a bedroom, and if we were making a noise or something he would come up to our room and whack us on the bottom or whatever. When he had gone, the pair of us would be laughing because he couldn't really dole out punishment, only when he was told to by my mother!

Kasper Schmeichel is a football oddity and a member of a select club where they can somewhat live up to the legacy of their footballing father. Malcolm and David Liddell would have no doubt been hamstrung by the pressure of their father's legacy as they grew up. Despite this, though, their sporting prowess was obvious very early. In a letter from Montgomery to Billy and Phyllis in January 1951: 'My word Malcolm and David are streets ahead of Campbell's James. He hasn't made an effort yet even to crawl, let alone walk.' Montgomery was comparing the progress of her grandchildren, and Billy's twins were already displaying a joy of being active at just ten months old.

The weight of being the son of Billy when playing football was immense. In his autobiography, Liddell described his normal week, and on a Sunday it was described that he would attend the football matches of his young sons when they were just over ten years old. He was rather disparaging about the hopes of his sons' chances of being professional footballers. David recalled:

> As a youngster you don't like reading things like 'far from being leading lights of their side'. To be honest I can only remember once him coming to a match that Malcolm and I were playing in. He didn't often come to see us play football because people would crowd around him but I remember after coming to see us play once, he said to me I spent more of the time on the ground, than I did standing up.

Malcolm also agreed with this feeling of footballing pressure when he said, 'He used to come and watch us, but he didn't have much faith in our ability.'

In the words of Malcolm on why he quit football:

> Quite honestly, I thought, I am never going to be as good as my father. I will try something different. I am sure that was the situation with both of us when we were younger. People thought we would be great footballers. I am sure it was the case with Kenny Dalglish's son Paul and Alex Ferguson's son Darren; they were good at football but not at the same level as their fathers.

The pressure of being Billy Liddell's sons is easy to imagine. The twins would always feel they were in the shadow of their father, particularly in football, so having to read the words doubting their ability would only lead to one of two avenues. Instead of seeking to prove their dad wrong, David and Malcolm would find their way in a different sport. They played tennis and went swimming together, rejoicing in the fact that they were better swimmer than their father. They would even compete against each other running up the hill by their house.

It was in basketball that the two found their sporting place though. They were more than competent players, Malcolm playing National League and for England once. David and his brother both represented two counties, Lancashire and Yorkshire, at basketball. Malcolm took it further than David, playing semi-professionally for Sunderland when they were in the National League.

Billy did not really understand the rules but was certainly proud to see his sons excel in a sport of their choice. The fact that they both became PE teachers also gave him great pride. Despite the possible simmering tensions and competition between the three, it was clear that the twins had a lot in common with their dad. They wanted to compete at a high level in sport, were well educated and educators of the younger generation. Malcolm perhaps best summed this up when he said, 'It is almost like our life journey had been decided by him.'

It is always easy to view a footballer and not think of the story off the pitch. Billy had so many different interests and this meant he brushed shoulders with celebrities, while passionately following his faith and partaking in charity work. All this while excelling in accountancy and in football. The death of his father turned his life upside down but brought him closer to his family.

Having said this, the words of his son would no doubt upset him. He had such a full schedule and set such an imposing example that he may have tipped the balance of work, free time and family time in the wrong direction. There seems little doubt that his heart was in the right place but possibly to the detriment of his twins.

The Men Who Put the Pool into Liddellpool – George Scott

George Scott – Liverpool FC (1961–1965)

When I knew Billy, I was only about 15 and I had only just arrived at Anfield as an apprentice and he was coming to the end of his career. I think I was only there for about a year or 18 months before he retired. He had time for everyone, considering what he had achieved. He achieved everything in the game, played over 500 times for the club and scored over 200 goals. Shankly told us all at the beginning that the club was called Liddellpool. He carried that team, there were some good players, but Billy was the main man. I would say he was one of the top three players that Liverpool ever had.

I've got a claim to fame, I scored a goal from a cross by Billy Liddell. We were playing at Melwood in the Lancashire League, it was for the C team, alongside Gordon Wallace, Bobby Graham, Tommy Smith, Chris Lawler and the others. We were getting warmed up at the start of the game with Everton C team and Billy was just standing on the line. It was a rainy sort of day and we were just warming up. Anyway, a ball went out to the wing and Billy had a raincoat on and he ran over and crossed it into the box and I headed it into the net. I said to the boys, 'I've scored a goal from a cross by Billy Liddell!' Well I will live on that forever and I'm still talking about it now, 55 years later.

He was a big star in the Scotland team. We all knew about Billy in Scotland, but we didn't know much about Liverpool to be perfectly honest because they were a Second Division team. They didn't have Shankly so the only thing of any note they had as far as Scotland was concerned was Billy. There was nobody else. He was very important to Liverpool though; he was an absolute legend, something like Steven Gerrard today. Everybody knew Billy and everyone revered him, he couldn't go anywhere in town without being stopped or mobbed.

He was always giving us young players encouragement, saying, 'You will make it son, you have got to be determined,' and Shankly loved that, because Shankly loved him. Shankly said, 'Listen to him boys, listen to him. He will give you good advice. Billy's done it and Billy's been there.' He used to give us all these talks and we were only kids, 15 and 16.

People will say, who was the greatest player Liverpool ever had? A lot of the modern boys will say it was Dalglish or it was Suárez, but if you look at a man who made

Liverpool known and was synonymous with Liverpool, achieved greatness at Liverpool with the club and internationally, Billy Liddell has got to be right up there. Especially with the conditions he played under, there were some good players in the team, but Billy was the main man. I would say he was one of the top three players that Liverpool ever had.

7

Creating a Liverpool Legacy

After the ball was centred, after the whistle blew.
Liddell got excited, up the wing he flew.
He crossed the ball to Stubbins; Stubbins scored a goal,
And left the poor old goalie, on his old banjo.
They laid him on a stretcher, laid him on a bed.
Rubbed his belly with cast-iron jelly, this is
what they said.
Liverpool are top of the League,
holding up the Cup!

THE ANFIELD roar had not truly found its singing voice until the early 1960s, soon after Billy's retirement. The combination of the top five songs in the charts being played through Anfield's public announcement speakers, popular bands such as, and none bigger than, Liverpool's very own Beatles, and the ever-increasingly fanatical fan culture, saw the Kop turn into a choir every other Saturday. The increasing fascination with Liverpool's singing culture attracted the BBC in 1964 and their words best describe the Anfield atmosphere:

> They don't behave like any other football crowd, especially not at one end of the Anfield ground, on the Kop. The music the crowd sings is the music that Liverpool has sent echoing around the world.
>
> It used to be thought that Welsh international rugby crowds were the most musical and passionate in the world, but I've never seen anything like this Liverpool crowd. On the field here, the gay and inventive ferocity they show is quite stunning. The Duke of Wellington before the Battle of Waterloo said of his own troops, 'I don't know what they do to the enemy, but by God they frighten me.' I'm sure some of the players here at the match this afternoon must be feeling the same way.
>
> An anthropologist studying this Kop crowd would be introduced to as rich and mystifying a popular culture as any South Sea island. Their rhythmic swaying is an elaborate and organised ritual. The 28,000 people on the Kop itself begin singing together, they seem to know intuitively when to begin. Throughout the match they invent new words, usually within the framework of old Liverpool songs, to express adoratory, cruel or bawdy comments about the players or the police. But even

then, they begin singing these new words with one immediate huge voice. They seem, mysteriously, to be in touch with one another, with 'wacker', the spirit of scouse.

The scenes that partner these amazing words are phenomenal and illustrate the fanatical passion of Liverpool supporters. This cannot have happened overnight. Liddell retired three years earlier; less than ten years earlier he was in his pomp and was the Kop's darling. The words that greeted the start of this chapter are possibly one of the earliest examples of a true Liverpool FC song.

Singing really entered fan culture around the 1958 Sweden World Cup (Brazil's World Cup-winning fanatical support inspiring English supporters) or possibly the 1962 Chile World Cup (again won by Brazil). For Liverpool fans, the signing of Ian St John in 1961 saw one of the first song adaptations as The Routers' song 'Let's Go' was sung in St John's honour in the early 1960s.

Supporters in more recent times have a repertoire of hundreds to roll through. The culture of Boss Nights with artists such as Jamie Webster, Kieran Molyneux, Timo Tierney and Ben Burke have seen hundreds and thousands of fans come together to sing their favourite Liverpool songs. Liddell again missed out on the best of this.

The words [p159] are sung to the tune of 'When Uncle Joe Plays the Rag on His Old Banjo', a song made famous in the US in 1912. The rerelease by Dick Thomas in 1945 brought it back into popular culture, so it was adapted by the Liverpool fans soon after their 1947 title success. Although not a song sung by an entire swaying Kop, it was an early example of the singing culture about to sweep Liverpool. Liddell's prominence in the tune, much like the 1950 FA Cup Final song, again illustrates his status.

Billy was the man, he was Liverpool, he was Liddellpool. He took the mantle from the great Northern Irishman Elisha Scott, the man who many attribute with having the first song from the Kop as the supporters would roar 'Lisha! Lisha!' Billy too was honoured to have this. Scott retired in 1934 and his legacy was not challenged until Liddell.

As mentioned, the crowd would not sing and sway like they did in the 1960s, but the Anfield roar was a spectacle. Once Liverpool won the ball and stormed towards the Kop, the crowd would move up and down the steps like waves in the sea, sucking the ball towards them. The screams of 'Give it to Billy!' would be echoed as the Kop wanted their man on the ball. The customary rattles in the hand of most supporters would be painted red and white, many inscribed with 'Liddell' or 'Liddellpool', in honour of the Kop's champion.

When Billy received the ball, the noise grew deafeningly loud, often followed by a signature drop of the shoulder and fierce shot. When the ball hit the back of the net, bedlam on Merseyside.

Much is made of the Kop's importance and it seems to be perceived as a later aspect of Liverpool's history, but this is not true. Speaking in 1949, then-Liverpool captain Jack Balmer wrote in Liverpool's 1949/50 season handbook about the duties of being the skipper:

> What are the duties of the man chosen to lead the team on to the field of play, who even now is walking to the middle in answer to the whistle? All important both to spectators and Management alike is what takes place on the field of play. If on spinning the coin, he has the good fortune to win the 'toss', choice of ends will, in all probability be a matter for the state of the weather to decide and also the knowledge that kicking into the 'Kop' for the second '45' may well mean pulling the game out of the fire. A few words with the men around him and the game is 'on'.

The fable of attacking the Kop in the second half is almost as long as the history of the club itself, at least dating to the Second World War. The crowd was fanatical and had a huge impact on the result of the match. With Billy as their hero, he had the biggest control over the supporters. He had the perfect combination of respect from team-mates, opposition, the board of directors and his loyal Liverpool supporters.

In 1955, Billy was given the distinct honour of becoming captain of Liverpool, after 17 years' service to the club. Such was his pedigree within the side that in the pre-season tour of France that preceded the campaign, he was asked by director T.V. Williams to join the committee to select the team for each match of the tour. Liddell even acted as an interpreter to speak with French railway staff to ensure that their kit could travel with them to that first match.

Laurie Hughes and Billy had been the oft stand-in captain for Bill Jones, grandfather of future Liverpool defender Rob Jones, before his sale following Liverpool's relegation to the Second Division. Liverpool-born Laurie took the role of captain for the 1954/55 season, but injury saw him miss the final few months of the campaign. Billy filled the role as captain. With Hughes now in his mid-thirties, Billy's fitness and performance consistency meant he fell into becoming the permanent captain, without any major fanfare.

Billy led by example, not a shouter and bawler but a hugely respected man. His presence would stiffen his team-mates into paying attention to his role on the pitch. Perhaps Billy's soft nature and lack of rousing speeches are what saw Johnny Wheeler awarded the captaincy in 1958. It must also be noted that Billy was 36 by this point, and although he was with the club for the next three seasons, his career was curtailing.

* * *

It seems unfair to squeeze Billy's Liverpool legacy into one chapter, but he was part of a time that truly did not deserve his presence. Bearing in mind that Liverpool were hot favourites for the double in 1950 (what would have been the first double in the 20th century) before the end-of-season capitulation that saw them finish eighth, performances continued to dishearten. Final positions of 9th, 11th, and 17th (where a final day win against Chelsea kept Liverpool in the First Division) followed before the disastrous 1953/54 season that saw Liverpool finish bottom of the league. Conceding close to 100 goals, the issues were obvious, and were in the opposite area of the pitch to Billy. Never one to shirk responsibility or blame and despite not being club captain at the time, Billy penned a letter to the press for the Liverpool fans, as an apology:

A team has a spell on top of the world and then it goes into the background for a while.

Liverpool have been very fortunate in playing in the premier division for 49 years. They have had their luck and their glory in these years 1904, 1905, 1914, 1922, 1923, 1947 and 1950.

Now 1954 is added as an inglorious date to the 'Red' calendar, but there is sure to be another date entered into the successes of the Anfield Men.

Whether it is 1955, or not, remains to be seen, but of this you can be sure, the players who don the red jerseys next year will be doing their best to make history repeat itself.

Unfortunately for the Reds, 1955 was not the season that Liverpool returned to the English top table. The Anfield faithful would have to wait until 1962 and Billy would not be part of the team that helped them do this.

As has been mentioned, Billy was painfully unlucky to not be part of the better teams that followed and went on to achieve reams of domestic and European medals. Instead, he made his legacy in *the worst* Liverpool team in history. This is not used as hyperbole; Liverpool were in the worst part of their history and still Billy stayed loyal. His legacy during this period is not medals, it is in the memories and glimmers of hope that he gave the fans. Instead of a chronology of events from 1950 to 1961, it seemed best to celebrate Billy's best moments that helped him create Liddellpool and secure his legacy at Anfield.

* * *

The last mention of Billy's Liverpool career came before the passing of his father. Evidence of Billy's professionalism and mindset was that in the first match after James's death, a 2-0 victory at home to Fulham, the *Liverpool Echo* wrote, 'Having written so often of Liddell's match-winning propensities and fighting spirit, one is almost stumped for something fresh to say about them. If Liverpool had three

Liddells in their attack, there wouldn't be a side anywhere to hold them.' People deal with grief in different ways, but Billy's way was taking control of his family and continuing to be a phenomenal footballer for Liverpool.

Billy was the idol of so many in Merseyside. As the years rolled by, the boys who had grown up watching and adoring him were now given the opportunity to play alongside him. One of those young men was Alan Banks, the Liverpool-born striker who went on to become a legend at Exeter City. He recalled, 'I made my full debut for Liverpool in September 1958, we played Brighton and had about 34,000 [fans]. Bill wasn't fit to play in that game, but he played in the following home game against Sheffield United and the crowd then was 44,000 people. That's the impact he had on the supporters at Liverpool.'

For Banks, as so many others, just being around Billy was an honour: 'It was the highlight of my whole career. I played for 20 years but playing and sitting next to Bill was absolutely incredible. I couldn't go any higher than having Billy sitting next to me.' Billy being part-time added to his mystique. The man who would only turn up two mornings a week, and on matchdays (after he had been in work from 9am–1pm that day and travelled to the match on the tram alongside supporters), but was supreme in his talents.

The question of who is the greatest of all time is so enthralling as there will never be an answer. Liverpool have had over 15,000 players in their history, so there will never be a way of saying X is by far the best player. However, there do certainly seem to be three major contenders for the crown: Steven Gerrard, Kenny Dalglish and Billy Liddell. What makes Liverpool's history so great is that the three never played together, so for this reason the argument splits generations of fans. Sadly, for Billy, many of his camp are dying off. The Kenny brigade are ageing, so Gerrard's fans may win the social media polls, but that does not seem the best way to decide.

There could be a whole book, never mind a few paragraphs in a chapter, devoted to who is the best. Personal opinion aside, it would be remiss not to mention that every person, every single one, that was asked the question of who the best is of the three, answered Liddell. Whether it was because they had spent the past hour reminiscing about the man before the question or not, this cannot be ignored.

His peers and comparable players are certainly Stanley Matthews and Tom Finney. Liverpool, Preston North End and Blackpool or Stoke City fans will all have their own opinions on the Liddell/Matthews/Finney debate. One thing for certain though, the supporters in this era were lucky to be able to witness three great wingers ripping up defences weekly. A lot of comparisons are also drawn with George Best when discussing Billy, although the two could not have been more different off the pitch. This again helps build a picture of the influence Billy had on his team.

The main point to come from that is not that Billy is the greatest, or that the people who wanted to help with the research for the book thought he was the best. The thing to note again is that the players of the past cannot be forgotten. Liverpool's 1990 squad were great and were considered so again when Liverpool won the league in 2020. England's 1966 team became significant when England lost the 2020 (21) European Championships Final. Cultural significance of a team or event can restore a legacy. It is important that the major events of the past are not forgotten and every opportunity to remember greats like Billy Liddell should be jumped upon, not just another mention of current players, but viewing current events through the prism of significant events of the past.

* * *

Countless goals have been mentioned by the loyal supporters, team-mates and family members during the research for this book. Milestones and important goals will always be important, but the ones remembered by those who held Billy dear are of more significance.

The lack of footage and success of this period means some are simply memories and legends, but this is all part of what Liddell is today. His days have passed and most memories are locked in the mind of those who watched him, wondering whether they remember certain matches and facts correctly but still rejoice in sharing the stories of their hero. This should not mean these stories are discredited, the mythology of Billy Liddell is what makes him so well remembered today.

One of the greatest of these memories is the numerous broken ribs, wrists and hands 'remembered' by supporters. What cannot be disputed from this is the power that Billy had in his boots. This was not fuzzy nostalgia of a past great, Billy had fire in his feet. One such example of this came against Derby County on a bitterly cold New Year's Day in 1955. Billy playing as number 9, was sent through on goal and unleashed a characteristic cannonball shot on target and it appeared to most that keeper Terry Webster had saved well. However, Webster was soon seen staggering, barely making it through the first half without collapsing. Other than again showing the poor health and safety protocol for players, the sheer force of a Liddell shot and an icy leather ball incapacitated Webster. Jack Parry was forced to deputise in goal for the second half as Liverpool put two past Derby, Billy scoring the second on his 350th post-war league appearance.

It was not just opposition players that felt the force of a Billy piledriver – one young fan, John Kennedy, received a blow from a stray Liddell shot one matchday on the Kop. In this era, the reserve team would play at Anfield while the first team played away and vice versa. Supporters would either follow their team home and away, watch the first team and reserves on alternate weekends, or they would watch Liverpool and Everton, whose home matches also alternated. Towards the end of Billy's career, when he was getting fewer first-team opportunities in his mid-thirties, an incident occurred:

> I am pretty sure it was the 1959/60 season, I've no idea who we were playing against but my dad and grandad were standing by one of the crush barriers behind the Kop. As you look at the pitch we were just to the left of the Kop, I guess about a third of the way back. The reserve games were fairly well populated, you would probably get about 5,000 every game and if Billy was playing it would be considerably more than that.
>
> Liverpool were kicking into the Kop end and Billy had his shot during the game. I don't remember the shot, I just know he hit it and the ball went slightly to the left of the goal, over the bar and came through and hit me on the thigh. I was sat on the crash barrier. I just remember the ball appearing and crashing on to my leg. Of course, I screamed the place down. I was around four years old and I felt like I had been killed!
>
> I remember Billy moved to the front of the wall at the Kop and was about to jump in but my dad and grandad stopped him. They said, 'It's okay Billy, he's fine.' Well I wasn't fine, I was crying my leg off! They were going, 'Billy, Billy, he's fine,' and my

old fella shouted, 'He won't wash his leg for a week Billy, he'll be made up with this!' Billy went, 'Are you sure?' and they said, 'Yes, he's fine.'

Billy didn't actually get in the Kop, as I've read elsewhere, but he was definitely prepared to. He was going to jump in the Kop, which is the measure of the man that he thought it appropriate to come and look after this little fella who had been hit with a ball.

Billy also scored spectacular goals. In 1956 he scored two in a minute to dump Accrington Stanley out of the FA Cup at Anfield. His first, a bullet header from outside the box that rebounded off the underside of the bar, lived long in the memory of the 48,000-plus crowd present. The second goal came in the same minute, just one of the 32 in his greatest scoring season for the Reds. Against the same opposition in the following year, Billy scored two in the very rare event where the Reds wore gold jerseys. Due to poor visibility on a January afternoon, gold jerseys were selected to improve the vision of the players.

Remembering again the terrible playing standards on offer, Billy being a wide man would be tasked with carrying the ball through the thick mud. As the goalmouth and centres of the pitch were often the worst affected areas, Billy would target the rare patches of green on offer and use them as the space from where he would loft in his delicious crosses, begging to be put home.

In 1954, at the height of Liverpool's demise, Billy was part of a team drubbed 9-1 away to Birmingham City. For Billy to shine on this day is again telling of his talents. The pitch was the terrible combination of soft on top and rock hard underneath. Billy managed to collect the ball on the icy surface, spin and produce a famous drive at goal, which flew past the keeper in a true showing of Billy's great power from outside the box.

His two goals against Grimsby Town are fondly remembered by one supporter, Paul McNulty:

> The first thing I remember of him, I was only nine at the time, it was the first match of the season in 1958. Billy Liddell scored two, the first one was a penalty and Jimmy Melia got the other. It was the first time I had been to a game of my own, the ground was chocker [47,502]. Previously either my dad or other people took me and you could walk around to both ends, to the Anfield Road via the Kemlyn Road and then you would swap at half-time in those days. But that day you couldn't because it was so busy. Billy had a cracking game and I'll always remember the crowd after his penalty, everyone loved him.

An interesting aside that did come up around the name Liddellpool was its negative reception from some supporters.

They were offended because it suggested that Liverpool were just Billy Liddell. They wanted to ensure the other players were respected. Liddell may have acted as a one-man-band for many, but there were always ten others for the loyal fans to support.

It has been asserted that the phrase was often used by Everton supporters to ridicule their struggling neighbours. Yes, Billy was good, but it was all they had, and not good enough to get them out of the second tier. Despite the many fond connotations of the nickname today, some were offended when it was used in defence of their other heroes on the pitch.

What is certain is that Billy's importance to the team was monumental; everything revolved around him. The chat from supporters through the week would be, 'Do you think Billy will be fit for the weekend?' It was a matter of life and death whether he played or not. When they found out that he was playing it would give the red half of the city a palpable lift, the impetus to get through the week knowing that they now had a better chance of winning the match, because he meant so much to them.

From 1954 onwards, it is fair to say that Billy carried the team. There were jokes that the supporters and the board did not want to get promoted as they knew they were not good enough for the First Division. Billy carried the side so much and, other than the first disastrous Second Division campaign, Liverpool did flirt with promotion most seasons but just fell short in the end. The supporters knew that coming close was mainly down to Billy, and without him they would be nowhere and certainly not of a standard to hold their own in the First Division.

Individual performances are perhaps best remembered for strikers when they receive the match ball in return for scoring three goals in the same match. Billy did this on five separate occasions (Tottenham 1951, Fulham 1954, Ipswich 1954, Nottingham Forest 1955, Blackburn 1958). The first, and only time in the First Division, came away to Tottenham in December 1951. The fantastic team performance saw Liverpool run out 3-2 winners with Billy scoring all the Reds' goals. This was another match where Billy received a substantial head injury, at the hands of Alf Ramsey, following a clash of heads. Billy, of course, played on and scored his first, a tap-in, inside ten minutes. Next came a fine Bob Paisley cross, tucked home by Billy to make it 2-0. Spurs fought back to 2-2, but Billy was like a man possessed to get his team back in front, finding himself one-on-one before being hacked down by the future England manager and knight of the realm, Ramsey, inside the box. Billy scored the resulting penalty and Liverpool went on to win the match.

Again, the lack of footage in the day also meant that many opposition supporters, particularly the ones in the Second Division and FA Cup, would be unaware of Billy's talents until he played against them. One example of some ill-informed opposition support came from Liverpool fan, Adrian Killen:

One of my first away games was at Blackburn Rovers. Them days the fans used to mingle and there was no segregation. So, I'm on a crossbar [crush barrier] and obviously my dad is behind me and there were these two Blackburn fans chatting.

'Here Stanley, I don't think much of this here Billy Liddell, do you?'

Anyway, about a minute later, Billy cuts in on to his right foot and bang! Right in the top corner past Blackburn's goalkeeper. I remember that fella then saying:

'Here Stan, did you see that!?'

Anyway, Billy goes on to score a hat-trick and I always remember it was what they call a genuine hat-trick – right foot, left foot and header. I will always remember the faces of those two blokes after the game. I think they thought more of Billy Liddell after that!

Billy's rise to stardom is hard to compare to many previous stars. If his era of fame feels far away now, the club legends during his playing days feel almost prehistoric when viewed anachronistically. The late 1950s/early 1960s Anfield housed a legend in Ephraim Longworth. Eph was the left-back for

Liverpool in the 1920s, his career spanning 18 years. He had the distinction of being Liverpool's first-ever captain of the English national team when he was given the job in only his second appearance. When he was in his seventies, he would spend time with current players underneath the old Main Stand. Anfield had a snooker table and this club legend used to love his snooker. Despite his shaking hands, the Liverpool captain for the 1914 FA Cup Final would destroy most of those who dared challenge him.

The purpose of this story illustrates how Liverpool legends were treated in their later years. The club obviously held the Bolton-born defender in high regard and were happy for him to spend time with the current squad. However, he was not honoured or respected as he should have been. Billy never had the opportunity to reach the age of Longworth and the club failed to truly honour both men in their lifetime.

One major feat that was achieved by Billy was breaking another legend, Elisha Scott's, appearance record for Liverpool. The accomplishment was honoured when Billy equalled the achievement in November 1957 at home to Notts County. Billy, of course, was on the scoresheet. He scored the third in a 4-0 victory on a landmark day. It was honoured by the *Liverpool Echo*, which depicted Billy atop the Liver Building, in place of the Liver Birds. The report dedicated to him wrote: 'There are too few players of the calibre of Liddell, on or off the field. The game would be the better for more of them.' The Liverpool board recognised this moment by presenting Billy with a radiogram, a cocktail cabinet and a china cabinet. The Liverpool Supporters' Club gave him a portable typewriter. On the field, he was presented a bouquet of flowers by the Notts County team, presumably for him to take home to Phyllis!

Despite the personal acclaim that will always come with an exploit such as an appearance record, this was never what Billy strived for. His goalscoring feats are something that will ensure his legacy lives on. Football is perceived to have started in 1992 and only Premier League records count, apparently. However, when the likes of Mo Salah break all the club Premier League records available, the 100 years that preceded Sky's birth of football suddenly matter again.

One great example of this is George 'Dod' Allan, the Scot whose name returned to headlines in 2018 as Salah became the second-quickest man to reach 30 Liverpool goals. The fastest was Allan, in 1896, and he managed to fit a lot of goals into his short Anfield career, 56 in 96 Liverpool matches. The man from Linlithgow was famous for his duels with the well-known keeper 'Fatty' Foulke but Allan sadly passed away in October 1899, aged just 24. Allan deserves to be remembered for this feat. Whether it happens in the 1800s or 2800s, it should be remembered.

Billy has two avenues through which his personal feats will be remembered best, two of the most significant: goals and appearances. At the time of writing, Billy sits 12th in all-time appearances and fourth in goals, another important time to mention the years taken from him during the war. If his wartime statistics for Liverpool alone are added to his tally, he would have 154 more matches and 83 extra goals, which would make him the fourth-top on appearances and second-top goalscorer. The fact he still had time to fight in a war and represent other teams within these statistics only suggests that he would have managed more matches and goals, finding himself even higher in the charts. All this while not training full-time due to his job as an accountant.

These accolades mean that every time a player closes in or surpasses Billy's numbers, his name will return to the headlines and significance again. With player loyalty seemingly decreasing with each year that passes, it seems likely that Billy will remain high on the list and thus his legacy will increase as it becomes progressively clear how significant and rare his achievements are.

Despite all of this, Billy was never in football for personal glory. In the words of his son, David: 'I don't think personal records and accolades were important, he played because he loved the game. He was a lay preacher as well, so he played the game for God really.' Whether he wanted it or not, Billy will always live on with Liverpool FC, thanks to his phenomenal personal statistics.

There has been a conscious effort to try to mention as many examples of head injuries as possible, when relevant, to highlight the possible links between dementia and football, especially the use of the old, heavy leather balls. Another example of Billy playing through head injury came against Doncaster Rovers in 1956. He had received a large gash from a clash of heads with Charlie Williams, and the set-up of Easter fixtures at the time saw the same teams face each other on Good Friday and Easter Monday, so Williams was to return to Anfield. Upset with his clash with their main man, the Anfield crowd was on the back of Williams. The *Liverpool Echo* wrote in dated and discourteous vocabulary, 'Williams who is a coloured boy, was sticking closest to Liddell.'

The close marking of Williams caused another clash of heads, meaning Billy had to have his large head bandage re-strapped. During the treatment, a dinner knife was thrown towards Williams from the Kop amidst the racist remarks being aimed at the defender. Williams, who went on to become a comedian in later life, picked the knife up and feigned being stabbed before dramatically falling to the floor. The Kop returned with laughter and the barrage of abuse towards Williams ceased, his quick and comical thinking winning over the supporters. This is, of course, an upsetting example of a supposedly bygone era where racism was as much a part of football as it was of society. Although this certainly has not changed enough since then, another example of a black man having to go above and beyond to be treated the same as a white man illustrates the lack of major progress in modern society.

Billy's glory days have been examined in detail, and to gloss over the periods of Second Division obscurity would be careless. In fact, the calamitous state of the club could be attributed as securing Billy's legacy as it made him appear better for being around such bad players. If Shankly is thanked for getting Liverpool out of the mire, and Liddell forgiven for not being able to do any more, then who was to blame?

Following the resignation of George Kay through ill health in 1951, two men were tasked with getting Liverpool promoted back to the big time, before Shankly's arrival in 1959. These were Don Welsh and Phil Taylor. The fact they did not achieve their ultimate goal means at least some blame must be placed on them.

Don Welsh was an intelligent man who arrived at Anfield from Brighton. He was a big personality who had a good playing career with Charlton Athletic. He knew the game and made Anfield a lively place with his vigour and ability to speak to players and join in training. He went on to be more a cheerleader than a master tactician, but the players loved playing for him. Some questionable signings were certainly to blame for Liverpool's relegation lack of progress, but how much say Welsh had in these is uncertain.

He did oversee two great FA Cup matches at the Reds. In a 1952 FA Cup fourth-round tie at Anfield, Welsh's tactical tinkering caused havoc with the travelling Wolves team, managed by Stan Cullis. The plan from Cullis had been to mark Billy out of the game, with Billy Wright to stand on the outside-left Liddell. However, as the match kicked off, Billy and Cyril Done switched positions. Billy, despite wearing number 11, played as centre-forward and hoodwinked the opposition. Billy assisted Paisley for the opening goal and Done scored the second in a 2-1 victory, masterminded by Welsh.

Another FA Cup fourth-round match to be remembered was the 4-0 victory over Everton at Goodison Park. Some 70,000 attended to see Second Division Liverpool, without an away win all season, travel to First Division Everton across Stanley Park. Centre-forward Liddell put Liverpool ahead, calmly bringing the ball down in the box, flooring the defender with his right-foot touch, then putting it past Jimmy O'Neill with a great left-foot finish. Liverpool did not stop there, with Alan A'Court and a John Evans double ensuring it was a derby day to remember. Laurie Hughes was at centre-half for the Reds but got injured, so Billy was placed at centre-half for the remainder of the match and was tremendous.

Yet Don Welsh will forever be the man who took Liverpool down to the division they so struggled to return from, defeat to Blackpool in 1954 cementing the first relegation for 50 years. The 1954/55 campaign that saw Liverpool defeated 9-1 by Birmingham and finish 11th meant Welsh's days were numbered. His contract was ended by mutual consent at the end of the following campaign.

The man selected to take the helm was Phil Taylor, the former 1950 FA Cup Final captain and England international who racked up over 300 official Liverpool appearances between 1936 and 1954. He was well versed in the club, how it was run and in the First Division glory days.

On the whole, Taylor advanced the club. Smart signings of Tommy Younger and Johnny Wheeler, partnered with high league finishes, helped his claim to the hotseat. However, they were becoming the nearly men too often, always falling short of promotion without a huge chance of achieving it. He was a lovely man and respected by the players, but the overbearing board involvement belittled his grip over the club. Shankly came in and stood up to them, demanding change and control. Whether Taylor could ever truly have done that is uncertain. He tried to advance the club but the board did not facilitate this.

It seems harsh to boil his whole managerial career down to one match, but with Taylor it is necessary. In January 1959, Liverpool travelled to Worcester City, the first FA Cup tie Billy had missed since the end of the war. They had travelled to Worcester the Saturday before but the match was cancelled because the field was not in a good enough condition. The Reds returned on the Thursday and the field was just as bad, if not worse. It was iced over and really should have never been played on. The playing surface evened everything out and the Liverpool players were not prepared for it. Despite eight of Worcester's team being in work that morning, the Southern League side beat Liverpool 1-0, and that was the end of Phil Taylor.

Taylor was a real gentleman and a very good player, and he was trying to change things within the club. This result was enough though. It was akin to the embarrassment brought to the club by the 1953 defeat away to Gateshead, in which Billy was part of the team, a result that damaged Welsh's grip on the job. Taylor was now close to the exit door, with a certain Bill Shankly coming the other way.

* * *

The overarching Liddell legacy today seems to boil down to three things. The team being known as Liddellpool, him and Stanley Matthews being the only players to represent Great Britain more than once, and his goal that never was against Manchester City in 1956.

In the round before the famous FA Cup tie with Manchester City, Billy had managed to keep the tie alive after he scored his second in the final seconds of the match against Scunthorpe with a tremendous header, taking the match to a replay at the Old Show Ground. Billy spearheaded the victory over the Third Division side with a goal and an assist, setting up the Man City match in the fifth round, which finished 0-0, despite a highly contentious Liddell goal ruled out for offside. They headed to Anfield for the replay.

The cup acted as a reminder of past glories for Liverpool during this period and often attracted the largest gates in

Second Division seasons. On that February Wednesday afternoon (the days before floodlights enabled midweek evening matches) over 57,000 were in attendance on a day so cold that kids were building ice blocks in the streets, to witness a moment synonymous with Billy's career: 'Twenty years hence, though I shall not be here, my successor will probably still be answering readers' questions about the gallant Liddell goal which was 15 seconds too late to produce a period of extra time.' The *Liverpool Echo* was close, as now over 60 years since the day, the match remains contentious.

With two minutes left in the match, Liverpool and Man City were level 1-1 after nearly 180 minutes of football over two matches. With just one minute remaining, Lancashire-born Joe Hayes put City ahead, despite the match seemingly being destined for extra time. Then came the controversy.

Sandy Griffiths became vilified on the red side of Merseyside, much like Clive Thomas in 1977 and Pierluigi Collina in 2005 became for the blue half, and was never to referee Liverpool again following this match. There were mere seconds left when Griffiths claimed that both his linesmen had signalled to him that the match should have ended. He blew his whistle at 45 minutes and 15 seconds of the second half. Only 15 seconds were added on despite injuries and three goals occurring during the period. Clearly paying more attention to his stopwatch than the action, Griffiths blew his whistle just as Billy carried the ball from the halfway line on a snow-dressed Anfield turf and unleashed a 35-yard thunderclap that nearly broke the net. Despite the ball flying into the goal past Bert Trautmann and sending the crowd into a frenzy, the whistle had signalled the end of the match before the goal was scored. Or had it?

The legend of the goal will be forever remembered because of the lateness of the non-goal and the controversy that surrounded it. This hullabaloo did not fully come to the fore until the following day as the *Liverpool Echo* published its 'Dramatic Liddell Picture'. Despite Griffiths claiming that Billy was 15 seconds too late, the image of the referee with his arm in the air after the ball had left Billy's right foot put this into dispute. The drama and folklore surrounding this moment has made it a favourite tale of the Second Division days.

Further legend around the goal grew after stories circulated that City skipper Roy Paul was giving the referee a lift home to Wales, so he did not want a period of extra time, as he could get home earlier. Griffiths had a Clive Thomas-esque reputation for wanting to make the game about themselves, the referee, rather than just officiating. This thirst for attention and the apparent meter running on his lift to Wales have only added to the legend of this famous event.

Due to the match being played on a Wednesday afternoon, the crowd was full of work- and school-dodging, or sagging, supporters and the mischievousness of their attendance has no doubt built the mystique around the match and 'goal'.

Even with Billy's humble nature, due to the fact he would be asked about this goal so often, he admitted it was a great finish when it came up in conversation. The fact that City also went on to win the FA Cup that season, further cements the legend around the day.

Many of the fans present had not heard the whistle that followed Billy's 'goal', so remained in the ground in anticipation of the extra-time period that was to follow. In a hope to empty the ground, there had to be an announcement over the tannoy to confirm that the match had finished 2-1 and Liverpool were out. Griffiths was lucky that he had managed to leave the pitch before many were made aware of his controversial decision!

* * *

The only question that can really remain with Liverpool and Liddell, is why did he stay? This certainly was not an era of money-chasing players, mainly because of the wage cap of £20 that was in place. However, personal success and accolades must have been an incentive for many players. Nobody enjoys playing in a team below their own standard, and Billy was above Liverpool and the division they were in.

He would not have been alone in his pursuit of trophies if he had chosen to leave Liverpool. One example is someone who would share a Great Britain dressing room with Billy, John Charles. The Welshman, much like John Watson's transfer to Real Madrid in 1947, moved to Juventus in 1957.

The two saw the lure of the chance of success abroad as big enough to leave their homes and take a chance. The lack of wage caps in certain countries would also have provided Billy the opportunity to earn more money for his family.

The truth is, no one will know for sure why, but it is possible to make a fair guess. Billy had been at the club since before the war, he had met his wife and now rehoused his whole family in the city. His humble nature would have meant that he did not need trophies; money would certainly have helped though. The guaranteed job in accountancy was probably as big a factor as anything else. Life after football was a financial consideration for players in this era. The club had been good to Billy and he was loyal in his nature, he was not for sale and never wanted to leave.

Creating a Liverpool legacy is not an easy feat, and Billy did it without asking for it. Liddell made Liddellpool through performances, important goals, ghost goals, personal accolades and loyalty. No one event creates a legacy, but over 20 years of service and prodigious performances certainly helps and that is how Liddell became the main man of Anfield.

The Men Who Put the Pool into Liddellpool – Gordon Wallace

Gordon Wallace – Liverpool FC (1961–1967)

I would have been about 15½, my first season was Billy's last. My first memories of him were my landlord telling me that the team used to be called Liddellpool because he was pretty much a one-man band. Even at that age, from the recollection I have, he was such a powerful man, and I can understand why people used to tell us as kids about Billy Liddell and how powerful his shooting was. He could head the ball, he kicked with his left and right, he had everything.

We met each other as he knew my father Dougie Wallace, as they had played together for Scotland. He mentioned the fact in asking how my father was and he made sure to come over to me very early on having been there. I hadn't really heard of Liverpool and Liddell. But then people started talking when you're there about Liddellpool rather than Liverpool, and you stand there talking to a 38-year-old man who was a legend at the club.

My dad would always ask how Billy was, and I would just say he was fine, and he'd pass on his best wishes and likewise my dad would send them to him. My dad was at Clyde while Billy was at Liverpool, so they'd only played together at international level, but he had a lot of respect for him.

Well, I always remember the game where he hit a 25-yarder and the goalkeeper went to catch it, the power of it took the keeper over the line and into the back of the net. I can't remember the team but what I can remember is what a gentleman he was, my high regard for his footballing skills, which goes without saying and, of course, when I was about 15 or 16 they were known as Liddellpool. They are the things that have stuck in my mind. I saw him in training and his power even then at 38 years of age was just incredible, how strong the man was, so he obviously looked after himself over the years. Apart from that I can't really say a lot more.

The supporters idolised the man, absolutely idolised the man. He used to get on the bus and sit there with them and walk up with the fans. He was just like any other working man, it just happened to be as a professional footballer. I am sure that was why he was well respected in the city.

8

Scotland and International Career

IT HAS been said enough times that the disparity between struggling in the Second Division with Liverpool and Billy's talents was colossal. In the face of being surrounded by substandard team-mates and tasked with pulling Liverpool through the worst period in their history, Billy remained loyal and his aptitude shone through. The best depiction and reward for this was his international career.

Playing international football as a Liverpool player in Billy's time was a rarity, in fact of his 93 Liverpool first-team team-mates, only 11 managed to represent their country while they were at Anfield:

- Roger Hunt – England (34 Apps, 1962–1969)
- Tommy Younger – Scotland (24 Apps (16 at LFC), 1955–1958)
- Gordon Milne – England (14 Apps, 1963–1964)
- Cyril Sidlow – Wales (7 Apps, 1946–1949)
- Alan A'Court – England (5 Apps, 1957–1958)

- Ray Lambert – Wales (5 Apps, 1947–1949)
- Laurie Hughes – England (3 Apps, 1950)
- Phil Taylor – England (3 Apps, 1947)
- Gerry Byrne – England (2 Apps, 1963–1966)
- Bill Jones – England (2 Apps, 1950)
- Jimmy Melia – England (2 Apps, 1963)

Billy was part of a select club of Liverpool players that managed to represent their international team during this period, just 12 per cent of players. The omission of Matt Busby is due to the fact he only played with Billy during the war, and wartime international fixtures are also not included, which is why Willie Fagan is missing. Nevertheless, this adds extra merit to the 29 peacetime and eight wartime Scotland caps won by Billy.

This number is only bettered by Roger Hunt, a man whose international career began after Billy's retirement while he was part of the Shankly Liverpool team lifting themselves out of the Second Division and into the success that followed. Billy was head and shoulders above his team-mates and this statistic alone illustrates his importance to his two homes – Liverpool and Scotland. He was also helping spread the word and image of Liverpool through his performances, no doubt making it a more desirable destination for budding Scottish players, like *The Lost Shankly Boy*, George Scott, who would have the opportunity to train with the great Billy Liddell in future years.

It felt best to examine this away from the sphere of Merseyside, as this is what Billy's Scotland career was. Being selected for Scotland was a huge honour. Doing so as an English league player was a feat, but someone plying their trade in the Second Division of English football and still receiving the call-up was almost unheard of.

Billy also had the honour of representing Great Britain during this period. In what is probably the most widely known and quoted Liddell fact, he and Stanley Matthews are the only players to represent Great Britain more than once. These matches will be examined further, but the reasoning behind this fact should be explained.

The formal presence of the English, Welsh, Scottish and Northern Irish Football Associations prevented a United Kingdom and a Great Britain football side. All four nations readily competed against each other in Home Nation tournaments, which ensured separation, rivalry and individualism for all four countries.

Early participation in Olympic Games saw the Great Britain team entered in 1908 being made entirely of English players and referred to as an English team by many. The English FA continued to select solely English players for the next few Olympics before only amateurs could be included. So, these teams are never thought of as either British or a selection of the best players in the UK.

The 2012 Olympics was possibly the closest to a Great Britain team since that era. After much apprehension from supporters and the four Football Associations, the team came together. There was a select number of overaged players allowed so most were under 23. With Euro 2012 in the same summer, anyone participating in that tournament did not play in the Olympics. This again proved to be a team that did not represent the best of British football, due to the Olympics being described as not being the pinnacle of a British player's career, and the team has not met up since.

There were also two friendlies between Wales and the Rest of Britain in 1951 and 1969, as well as the celebration of the European Economic Community, which saw Britain join forces with Ireland and Denmark to face a team comprised of players from West Germany, Belgium, the Netherlands, Luxembourg, France and Italy in 1973. However, again these are not examples of England, Scotland, Wales and Northern Ireland competing together as a united team, chosen from the best players available.

What Billy Liddell and Stanley Matthews achieved by participating in the 1947 and 1955 Great Britain teams was establishing their pedigree and longevity in British football. As there has been no direct competing or comparable teams other than the two occasions during this eight-year period, Liddell and Matthews deserve the honour of this unique statistic.

* * *

The first wartime international matches for Billy have already been discussed, so their ineligibility to his records do not need to be mulled over again. Instead, his Scottish career will be analysed from his 'first' cap in May 1946 up to his final cap in 1955.

Although Billy was an honorary Scouser, he was a very proud Scot. His involvement in Scottish culture within Liverpool only further exemplifies this. Football took Billy from Fife to travels around the world, although never in a major competition.

Scotland have not participated at the World Cup since 1998. Since then, they have failed to qualify for five consecutive World Cups and have only played in eight of the 21 iterations of the competition (up to the 2018 Russia World Cup). Many members of the Tartan Army would give an arm and a leg to see their side play on the greatest stage again; however, they were once able to reject the opportunity to do so. Scotland qualified for the 1950 World Cup in Brazil but, nevertheless, decided not to play.

Billy's best chance of playing in a World Cup was probably in 1950, at the age of 28. Scotland and England both qualified through the Home Championship as the top two teams, but the SFA did not accept the offer to participate. To fully understand why Scotland chose to do this, the history of the British Home Championship must be delved into. Scotland, England, (unified) Ireland and Wales had withdrawn from FIFA in 1920. They felt uneasy about playing against First World War rivals, as well as not enjoying a growing foreign influence in the British game.

This gave the Home Championship a huge boost of significance as it became the main form of international competition for all the British sides. Between the two wars, Scotland won the competition 11 times, Wales seven, England seven, and none for Ireland. Scotland were the dominant side during this period, and it is unfortunate for them that they were not able to display this on the world stage, especially in its modern format and stature. This illustrates how competitive the tournament was. In 1937 the British Home Championship match between Scotland and England at Hampden Park attracted over 147,000 supporters. Despite missing out (through choice) on Uruguay 1930, Italy 1934 and France 1938, the British teams were enjoying their own international tournament. The huge number of supporters at the Scotland vs England match in 1937 is even more impressive when it is compared to the 45,000 fans that attended the 1938 World Cup Final between Italy and Hungary.

The success of the British Home Championship was undermining the importance of the FIFA World Cup by the start of the Second World War. If FIFA truly wanted a World Cup, then they knew they had to find a way to tap into the passion and ability displayed in Britain. Following the end of the war, FIFA tried to get the British nations to re-join the governing body. As a bargaining tool, they offered a guaranteed slot in the 1950 World Cup to the winners of the British Home Championship. This was a very generous offer and helps to illustrate the prestige of the competition at the time.

Other nations had to fight through rigorous qualification campaigns, playing matches across the globe, while the British teams were handed a relatively easy route to the finals. The British teams remained reluctant, so FIFA offered another qualification place to the runners-up, meaning that half of Britain was guaranteed the opportunity to play in Brazil 1950. An agreement was made, the British teams were to return to FIFA and World Cup participation. However, the SFA decided that should Scotland come second, they would not participate in the World Cup. They felt that if they had not proved themselves to be the best British team then they did not deserve the opportunity to play in FIFA's competition and contend to be the world's best. This heaped pressure on the Scottish team, who now knew that only a first-place finish would get them to Brazil.

Scotland went into the 1950 British Home Championship as reigning champions, and it was also the final time Ireland was represented as a unified nation. Ireland and Wales at this time were far from the quality of Scotland and England. Each team had to play each other once, and the Scotland vs England match was prescheduled as the final one of the tournament. The first round of fixtures saw Scotland beat Ireland in Belfast 8-2, and England beat Wales in Cardiff 4-1. Next, Scotland beat Wales 2-0 at Hampden Park, and England beat Ireland 9-2 in Manchester. Both Scotland and

England were guaranteed a top-two finish, and England had already confirmed they would be off to Brazil if they finished second, so all eyes were on Scotland to win their route to the finals.

A huge 133,191 supporters attended Hampden Park in April 1950, many in the hope of watching Scotland beat England. The Hampden roar was phenomenal in this era, the fanatical support of the passionate Scots perhaps best illustrated by the fact that close to 300,000 supporters in total attended two matches within a week at Hampden Park, for those between Scotland and England, and Aberdeen and Celtic.

Billy lined up for his eighth cap in Scotland's Willie/ Billy attacking line of Willie Waddell, Willie Moir, Willie Bauld and Billy Steel. Commentators at the time described it as 'more than an international, it's a cup tie with Rio and the World Cup the glittering prize'. Both sides battled hard throughout the match, with missed chances aplenty. England scored first but it was ruled out for offside.

Bert Williams, England's keeper, kept his side in the match with many great saves, and straight from one of them England went on the attack for Roy Bentley to put his side 1-0 ahead on the hour mark. Despite continued Scottish pressure, England held on to win. Scotland were afforded 'the glory of going down fighting' but they refused to go against their promise to not participate in the World Cup, despite encouragement from Billy Wright, England captain, for them to go to Brazil.

So that was that, Scotland had earned their opportunity to enter the premier international competition that they are today desperate to play in once again. England did not represent themselves brilliantly in 1950, and with defeat to Spain and a shock loss to USA following a goal from a Scottish emigrant, they were out. Scotland were not the only team to refuse participation in 1950. Despite desiring a 16-team tournament, only 13 contributed. Scotland joined France, Turkey, Austria, India and Argentina in refusing to travel, for differing reasons.

Scotland deserved their place in Brazil and could have been a strong team, and possibly a contender in the competition. However, they stood by their decision to miss out on an historic event – a decision that will likely never be repeated. There was certainly not the level of fuss at the time that there would be today. Perhaps most baffling of all is that Britain was offered the same qualification process for the next World Cup and Scotland again finished second; however, this time they chose to enter Switzerland 1954.

* * *

As has been mentioned, for Billy to be picked for the Scotland team, he faced competition from the likes of Lawrie Reilly, Willie Ormond, and Gordon Smith of

Hibernian (Eddie Turnbull and Bobby Johnston, the other two of the 'Famous Five' of Hibs also played for Scotland but were inside-forwards). So, it depended how the selectors saw the players, or what kind of player was needed. Reilly was a sniffer of chances in the penalty box, always sharp and alive, always aware. Willie Ormond had a bit of pace and a decent shot and maybe tried a few more tricks than Billy, but he was not as fast and direct. Gordon Smith was viewed as a graceful player to watch, and as good a crosser of the ball as Scotland has seen (the only player to have won a Scottish league championship with three clubs: Hibernian, Heart of Midlothian and Dundee). So that was some competition for Billy as they could all play the game.

The team was selected by committee, not a manager, with different club directors attempting to play their own players. Rangers and Celtic players were big crowd pullers, as were the players from the most popular English clubs. It was hard to be picked coming from a provincial club in Scotland, and Billy faced similar difficulty with Liverpool being a Second Division club for much of the time, making him less desirable to the selectors. Also, there was little continuity with squads as there was no one man with set ideas to pick the team. This caused a high turnover of players, and the fact that Billy had 93 Liverpool team-mates in his 534 matches and 69 Scottish team-mates during his 29 caps best exemplifies this. However, if you were playing well for your club you had a chance of being picked.

One of Billy's proudest Scottish moments came against England in 1951. The match contained another moment of Billy's bravery and head injury ignorance as he and Middlesbrough's Wilf Mannion competed for a header. Both were injured, Mannion much more so, though, as he was stretchered off with a broken cheekbone and covered in blood. Billy was attributed by some as ending the international career of Mannion, who only played one more England match after that day. Billy received a hefty knock to his head, hefty enough to break a cheekbone, but he again played on. Disregarding the potential long-term health issues, he certainly would have been glad he had the opportunity to do so.

Preceding the match, it had been discussed as to why Billy's goalscoring form of Liverpool had not transferred to the international stage: 'When I play for Liverpool I always seem to be in the thick of the game. When I play for Scotland, I feel tied to the wing for long spells; I lose confidence to try something on my own.' This is very similar to the goalscoring issues that met Billy's early Liverpool days as he felt constrained to remaining on the wing. His humble nature seemingly held him back but this honest self-assessment ahead of the match brought an ironic turn of events.

Over 100,000 supporters witnessed the final instalment of the 1951 Home Championship, looking to continue the Scottish run of being unbeaten at Wembley since 1934.

Following the Liddell and Mannion clash, England had to play the vast majority of the match with ten men. They battled well and took a surprise lead through debutant Harold Hassall, following some clever build-up play by Alf Ramsey and Tom Finney.

Billy dragged Scotland back into the match after his cross found fellow first-timer Bobby Johnstone before half-time and the sides went into the break level. Scotland started the next period like a different team, attacking from the off and scoring three minutes later through Lawrie Reilly. Six minutes later Billy pounced on a fumbled cross, his first-time right-foot volley finding the back of the net to put Scotland 3-1 up.

Tom Finney clawed England back into it, making for a nervy final half-hour. Despite pressure and penalty appeals, Billy's goal was enough, and he was happy to have returned to scoring ways. His goal came from his striker's instincts and by being in the box for the cross, clearly making a conscious effort to improve his attacking performance. His goal and assist on a great Scottish day proved that he was right to believe he could achieve more and motivated himself to do so.

Following the 1950 debacle and by 1954, Billy was 32, and by 1958 he was 36, so it is fair to assume this is why he was not selected for the World Cup in those years. He did not miss much in 1954 in Switzerland. Scotland's first-ever manager, Andy Beattie, resigned after only a couple of days, claiming to be in a hopeless situation with a squad of 13 players, including just one goalkeeper. All the other teams took the permitted 22 players. If Billy was deemed to not be in the top 13 Scottish players, he certainly would have been in the top 22 and should have had the chance to play in the World Cup. The terrible organisation and preparation were perhaps best depicted by the Scotland kits. They turned up with heavy shirts, socks and boots, and with no manager around, half-time consisted of taking your shirt off and standing in a cold shower for ten minutes! Not surprisingly, they were dumped out with two defeats in two matches.

There were some better Scotland matches ahead for the Tartan Army. The 1953 2-2 draw against England included a dramatic last-minute Lawrie Reilly equaliser at Wembley. They also experienced an opposite turn of events after they drew 3-3 with Wales at Hampden after being 3-1 up and absolutely in control of the match. However, Wales pulled back to 3-2, and then big John Charles broke away near the end and scored. There was a strong feeling that centre-half Willie Telfer should have brought Charles down to save the game, but he did not, and Telfer was never picked for Scotland again thereafter.

Billy was part of a three-match tour in Europe in the summer of 1955, alongside some great players, namely Dundee legend Doug Cowie. It was widely regarded as a successful tour and Billy played in all three matches. The first was a creditable 2-2 draw with Yugoslavia in Belgrade, next came the 4-1 win against Austria in Vienna and then a 3-1 loss to Hungary in Budapest. Against Austria the whole team was outstanding, helped by a first-minute goal from Archie Robertson. Cowie enjoyed a lot of the ball and managed a good supply to Billy, who slotted in the third in the 78th minute with a low shot into the left-hand corner. Although Austria scored with a deflected free kick in the 87th minute, fast-man Reilly scored again in the 89th to make it a great 4-1 result.

The match is remembered best for the hostile atmosphere in the crowd. Gordon Smith had been really turning it on in the second half, tormenting the left-back, and this annoyed the Austrians who soon resorted to some rough stuff. After the anticipated bad tackle, Smith made as if to retaliate, and the next thing spectators and military personnel were on the pitch. One fan headed directly towards Gordon and aimed a kick, whereupon Lawrie Reilly headed directly for the fan. The story goes that Reilly flattened the supporter, but Lawrie has since denied it. Although the situation could have been very ugly, the plentiful number of British troops around as well as the Austrians meant support was at hand.

The next match was in Budapest against the great Hungarian side that should have won the 1954 World Cup and who had already beaten England 6-3 at Wembley and 7-1 in Hungary. Confident after the performance in Austria, the Scots started well. The Hungarians were below par in the first half and Scotland led 1-0 at half-time. In the second half Hungary brought on two substitutes, including the famous centre-forward Nándor Hidegkuti, and they immediately played better, eventually going 3-1 up. Scotland were still in the match though, and were awarded a penalty not long after Hungary's third goal. Billy took the kick as he was the elder statesman in the team and was a regular penalty scorer for Liverpool. However, this time his kick was scrambled away by the goalkeeper, and although Billy then struck the post near the end with a shot from the edge of the box, it was all over at 3-1, a result seen as respectable, although of personal disappointment for Billy.

Ahead of the match in Hungary, the Scottish squad were travelling on the team bus to their hotel. There was unrest in Hungary at the time with the Soviets being in control of the country. There was a Romanian guide-come-interpreter on the bus with the squad whom the players, according to Doug Cowie, felt was really there to 'keep an eye' on them. He pointed out a statue that commemorated Russian soldiers who had lost their lives in taking over Hungary, whereupon Tommy Docherty piped up, 'What about the Hungarians who lost their lives?' Everybody else on the bus ducked their heads down behind the seat in front! Thereafter, there were serious conversations as to whether hotel rooms might have been bugged. It was only a year later that Ferenc Puskás and some others in the Hungarian team decided not to return to Hungary after Budapest Honvéd faced Athletic Bilbao in the European Cup. The home leg could not be played due to the Hungarian Revolution erupting in Budapest.

The England match at Wembley in 1953 was Liddell's 23rd. It was an exciting match for those in attendance, and when Sammy Cox, the Scottish left-back, was injured in trying to stop Tom Finney in the lead-up to England's second goal that put them ahead 2-1, it looked like game over. Cox was carried off with 20 minutes to go, and with there being no substitutions, Cowie was tasked with trying to cover Finney as a stand-in full-back as well as keep pushing up to support Steel and Liddell. However, Scotland managed to keep going forward and, in the last minute of the match, Reilly came to the rescue with a deserved equaliser despite the Scots being a man short.

Billy was lucky to travel the world and see so many different countries at a time when people did not go abroad often. The icing on the cake would, of course, be playing football at the same time – and playing with and against some great players.

During his international days amongst compatriots, Billy was still a member of the squad who spent his time on the periphery of the group. He was, as always, happier being in the background rather than in the limelight. In the changing room he would not be a shouter and swearer; he would more likely be sitting discussing the match with a similar type of character. Billy would rarely court friendships with Scottish team-mates and would certainly keep away from the louder members of the squads. He would never be someone doing a Lawrie Reilly, considering flattening a spectator! Even during trips, he would not be the man involved in any hijinks or be a late bedder at the bar drinking. He was what his grandfather had taught him to be, plain old Billy Liddell, a model professional.

He remained a proud Scot for the rest of his life and took his twin boys to watch Scotland face England at Wembley in 1975. The twins being born in England and representing England at basketball had less of an affinity to the Scottish team. Billy was Scottish through and through, so witnessing England win 5-1 would have really hurt him.

* * *

Scottish, Scouse and British – Billy had some memorable moments but only for three sides in his 'competitive' career. His Great Britain legacy began in May 1947 in the match coined 'The Game of the Century', as Great Britain lined up against the Rest of Europe. The seven-goal thriller certainly lived up to the billing, the context of the match being mentioned in relation to Liverpool's 1946/47 run-in, where participation and injury caused Billy to miss three of the final four matches of the season.

The match was played in Billy's native Scotland and the hype was building prior to the match. The *Daily Mirror* piled on the pressure by saying, 'On the shoulders of our players lies the responsibility of proving to the Soccer world that the teachers of the game are still better than the pupils.' Very much in the ilk of Skinner and Baddiel's 'Three Lions', the mission statement for the British players was protecting the 'origins' of football and proving that the Brits are the best.

The match coincided with the British sides' reinstatement to FIFA and was supposed to be held at the end of the campaign. However, the harsh winter of 1946 meant the match came in the midst of the end of the season for the Brits, none more dramatic than Billy's. The excitement and pride from Merseyside was perhaps best illustrated by the presence of four Liverpool directors at the match. Billy was putting Liverpool on the map ahead of them clinching the title.

Some 135,000 supporters were in attendance to see Wilf Mannion, Stanley Matthews and Tommy Lawton shine in a demolition of the Rest of Europe side. The fact that most of the British team played together either internationally or in the same league gave them a huge advantage over the patchwork Europe side. Nevertheless, the 6-1 scoreline demonstrated the dominance of the British and their successful defence of football, as it was seen. Wilf Mannion was credited with a hat-trick (some reports claiming one was a Parola own goal), Lawton with two and Billy Steel's 35-yard screamer was the pick of the bunch. Swedish star Gunnar Nordahl scored the only goal for the European side.

Billy played a pivotal role in the first goal of the day, linking up well with Billy Steel and Mannion, the man whose cheekbone he was to break four years later. Billy really took to Mannion during the trip and attempted to take him under his wing, and whatever Billy said worked, as Wilf was on fire. However, Billy's impact on the match was heavily hampered by the thigh injury he picked up before half-time, which ruled him out for two further matches, a big disappointment for this to happen in a match of such magnitude. Unaware of the problem, the *Sunday Post* wrote, 'Willie Liddell somehow or other gave me the impression he was not 100 per cent fit. Or was Willie a wee bit out of his class in such company?' This personal disappointment did not take away from the pride of being selected and the dominance of the British side.

Such acclaim is given to Liddell and Matthews and their participation in both famous matches, that it seems only fair to recognise the full squads involved:

Great Britain vs Rest of Europe, 10 May 1947

Great Britain – 1. Frank Swift (England, Manchester City), 2. George Hardwick (England, Middlesbrough), 3. Billy Hughes (Wales, Birmingham City), 4. Archie Macaulay (Scotland, Brentford), 5. Jackie Vernon (Ireland, West Bromwich Albion), 6. Ron Burgess (Wales, Tottenham Hotspur), 7. Stanley Matthews (England, Stoke City), 8. Wilf Mannion (England, Middlesbrough), 9. Tommy Lawton (England, Chelsea), 10. Billy Steel

(Scotland, Greenock Morton), 11. Billy Liddell (Scotland, Liverpool)

Rest of Europe – 1. Julien Da Rui (France, CO Roubaix-Tourcoing), 2. Poul Petersen (Denmark, Akademisk Boldklub), 3. Willi Steffen (Switzerland, Cantonal Neuchâtel), 4. Johnny Carey (Ireland, Manchester United), 5. Carlo Parola (Italy, Juventus), 6. Josef Ludl (Czechoslovakia, Sparta Prague), 7. Victor Lambrechts (Belgium, K.V. Mechelen), 8. Gunnar Gren (Sweden, IFK Göteborg), 9. Gunnar Nordahl (Sweden, IFK Norrköping), 10. Faas Wilkes (Netherlands, XerxesDZB), 11. Carl Aage Præst (Denmark, Østerbros Boldklub)

Great Britain vs Rest of Europe, 13 August 1955

Great Britain – 1. Jack Kelsey (Wales, Arsenal), 2. Peter Sillett (England, Chelsea), 3. Joe McDonald (Scotland, Sunderland), 4. Danny Blanchflower (Northern Ireland, Tottenham Hotspur), 5. John Charles (Wales, Leeds United), 6. Bertie Peacock (Northern Ireland, Celtic), 7. Stanley Matthews (England, Stoke City), 8. Bobby Johnstone (Scotland, Manchester City), 9. Roy Bentley (England, Chelsea), 10. Jimmy McIlroy (Northern Ireland, Burnley), 11. Billy Liddell (Scotland, Liverpool)

Rest of Europe – 1. Lorenzo Buffon (Italy, AC Milan), 2. Bengt Gustavsson (Sweden, IFK Norrköping), 3. Alfons van Brandt (Belgium, Lierse), 4. Ernst Ocwirk (Austria, Austria Wien), 5. Robert Jonquet (France, Reims), 6. Vujadin Boškov (Yugoslavia, Vojvodina), 7. Jørgen Leschly Sørensen

(Denmark, AC Milan), 8. Bernard Vukas (Yugoslavia, AC Bologna), 9. Raymond Kopa (France, Reims), 10. José Travassos (Portugal, Sporting CP), 11. Jean Vincent (France, Lille)

The first meeting in 1947 was a success and it had been mooted that the two would play each other ammually, but evidently this did not come to fruition, so the next and only other meeting between Europe and Britain was in 1955. The match was played in celebration of the Irish Football Association's 75th Anniversary, so was played in Belfast's Windsor Park. The British side donned the green Northern Irish strip (after wearing blue in 1947).

This remains the last occasion that all four home nations played together in a competitive fixture, with Stanley Matthews being the poster boy for Great Britain. Aside from Matthews, the team contained several iconic footballers. The home crowd would have been thrilled to witness local boys Danny Blanchflower and Jimmy McIlroy. The utility man John Charles was the principal Welsh representative, with Liddell gathering Scottish headlines for his second call-up, alongside Johnstone. The surprise omission of Tom Finney from both squads should be mentioned and is testament again to the supremacy of Liddell and Matthews.

The match was nothing like the previous meeting as the Rest of Europe swept Britain aside 4-1. Aside from goalscorer Jean Vincent and hat-trick hero Vukas, the Rest of Europe side boasted the great French forward, Raymond

Kopa. In 1956, Kopa joined Real Madrid and became part of one of the greatest club sides ever, claiming consecutive European Cups between 1957 and 1959, and included the Hungarian Ferenc Puskás.

Despite failing to greatly affect the match on a warm Belfast day with the playing surface closer to a public park than a football pitch, Billy was immensely proud to represent Britain again. The two plaques he was presented for each British appearance remained on display on his bookcase long after his retirement.

There is no doubt that Billy's international career was a story of what could have been, and that bizarre SFA decisions in 1950 and 1954 took his deserved World Cup chances from him. Had it not been for biased and ever-changing selection choices, he would also have had more caps for Scotland. Nevertheless, he could be proud of his international feats.

The British matches were exceptionally rare occasions to illustrate his status within football. Injury in the first match and a comfortable defeat in the second removed Billy's solid chance of being able to directly affect the outcomes. Having said that though, these two matches help mould Billy's legacy in football. The absence of piles of medals and international tournaments meant that this became one of his greatest achievements.

The Men Who Put the Pool into Liddellpool – Gordon Milne

Gordon Milne – Liverpool FC (1960–1967)

It's interesting because my hero was Tom Finney and I played with him at Preston. I also had the privilege of playing in Tom Finney's last game at Deepdale in 1960 before moving to Liverpool. My debut for Liverpool was in Billy Liddell's last ever game. Playing with and meeting Billy when I came to Liverpool showed me he was just as big a hero at Liverpool as Tom was at Preston.

The other similarity between the two was that they were both very talented in different ways, but very sincere and humble people. Billy was unassuming, he was helpful to young players and always talking to me in training in the short time that I worked with him. It's probably old-fashioned to say now, but he just came across as a proper gentleman and a wonderful ambassador for football, never mind what they did for the clubs.

They were two top players and admired. Billy was like Tom, not only admired for his achievements and what he did for Liverpool – he was admired nationally as a top player and a top person, and I think when the two go together, like it did with those two players, you have got the ultimate hero, haven't you?

I came to the team and I was just fresh out of the army, so I had not been training full-time with Preston. I came out of the army in May and joined Liverpool in the August, I think, or July, whenever it was, so I was a bit of a rookie, and at that time what I do remember is they had an ageing squad at Liverpool and I think Shankly identified that. There were a lot of senior players so it was difficult as a young newcomer. You felt a little bit alone at the beginning and the few occasions I came across Billy he was always asking, 'How are you?' and he knew my dad, Jimmy Milne, so he would ask, 'How is your dad?' so he made you feel comfortable in just talking to you. There were no airs and graces. Some of the other more senior players were a little bit more aloof and were a bit wary of a new young guy coming in and what he was going to be up to. But Billy wasn't like that at all.

9

Retirement and Bill Shankly

THERE IS no room for sentiment in football and all good things must come to an end. The decision for Billy to be dropped from Liverpool's first-team squad in October 1958 was taken for the first time in his 20 years with the club. His impact was remarkable, but time waits for no man and this day symbolised the beginning of the end of Liddellpool.

The 36-year-old was dropped by his former captain Phil Taylor, in the same season that Billy was relinquished of *his* Liverpool captaincy. The omission did, though, provide Billy with the chance to make his Central League debut for the reserves. The fact that Billy could reach 36 and never have been in doubt of starting a first-team match is another remarkable statistic of this strange time for him.

This immediately began talks of retirement, winding down and further scrutiny of every future appearance from the Scot. His pace, fitness, physique and finishing would forever be the topic of conversation whenever he pulled on the red shirt again. Taylor refused to comment on the situation as rumours of team-mate jealousy of Billy's preferential treatment for being part-time in training but full-time on the pitch began circling. This was a very rare moment of controversy around Liddell.

He certainly had not done anything wrong, other than ageing. Taylor's decision was bold and may have been a dressing room powerplay to show the other players who was in charge. The fact that Billy's playing career outlasted Taylor's managerial tenure may suggest how well this decision worked with the players and fans.

As early as 1950, an unexpected move to Bogotá, Colombia was touted. Neil Franklin and George Mountford from Stoke City, and Charlie Mitten from Manchester United had already signed for Independiente Santa Fe during the 'El Dorado' period of Colombian football. This was when Colombia pulled away from FIFA, so the foreign players and wage cap rules were removed from their game. This mainly attracted South American players, including Alfredo Di Stéfano, but Billy was also approached for a lucrative transfer. Huge signing-on fees were offered, which continued to rise with each rejection from Liverpool's loyal Scot. Rejecting Santa Fe and committing himself to his club, Billy commented, 'The disadvantage of leaving home, family and friends outweighed the financial benefits. All my interests are here at Anfield, and I should hate to leave.'

Now, with Taylor's exclusion of Billy, transfer rumours were reignited. Joe Mercer, the Arsenal 1950 FA Cup Final captain, tried to sign Billy for Aston Villa soon afterwards. The possible return to the First Division was quickly quashed by the board, who would not hear of losing their long-standing hero. This interest showed that Billy was still deemed good enough for the division above Liverpool, never mind the team he had carried for so many years.

Although Billy's power was decreasing and he was also losing his pace, the supporters were eager to voice their upset with the decision to drop their hero. So much so that in the following home match against Sheffield Wednesday, where Billy remained out of the limelight, the board had to issue the following statement in the matchday programme:

> In view of the doubts in the minds of our supporters due to certain newspaper reports with regard to the centre-forward selection for the match at Fulham, the Board think it right to break a silence of years regarding team selection.
>
> To commence with there are no greater supporters of Willie Liddell than the Members of the Board, both individually and collectively, but every player in the game eventually reaches the time when he cannot satisfy himself if playing every week without some relief. The greatest players of the game have shown the wisdom of a lighter programme of games in order that they can give their best and prolong their playing career. This position had to be faced

here last week and our readers can be assured that the action taken was believed to be in the interests of the player as well as the Club.

W. Liddell, J.P. (an honour correctly bestowed) is the greatest player the Liverpool Club has ever had and we look forward to his taking part in many more games in the red jersey.

The statement issued shows how big this issue was for the club. However, despite their words, Billy struggled to get himself back into the team again. The following season, he played in the October 1959 5-4 loss to Swansea Town, which saw Liverpool sitting 13th in the Second Division. It was to be his only first-team match for four months. When he was recalled on Valentine's Day's eve, it was under the stewardship of a certain Bill Shankly.

Such was the anti-Taylor opinion because of Billy being dropped from the side that the Anfield faithful gathered in the car park to lambast their manager. Billy had been out of the squad for four months, and in March 1959 another promotion looked to have slipped through Liverpool and Taylor's grasp. Angered with a 0-0 draw against Fulham, the supporters gathered in the car park situated in the Main Stand to chant, 'We want Billy!' Taylor was asking Billy to play as outside-right for the reserves, but the supporters believed he should be starting as centre-forward for the first team. Alan Arnell's performances were not up to the standard of Billy in the minds of most supporters, so the pressure was building on Taylor to return their hero to the starting XI. Despite his ageing body, declining speed and looming departure from the game, Billy was the main man for the Liverpool fans. They wanted him back where he belonged, on the pitch and pushing to get the Reds back in the First Division. Instead, this chance was not to be handed to him by Taylor, but by Shankly.

This was only Shankly's ninth match as Liverpool manager, and Billy was to play 11 of the final 14 matches of the new manager's maiden season. Some of the terminology used to describe his role in his penultimate match of the campaign perhaps best suggests his impact: 'Liddell, who has obviously lost his speed, did his best work in the second half, but close marking ensures that if he is not getting over the centres, there is little else to offer.'

It should be noted that this final spell of first-team action saw two famous moments for all those in attendance. One came against Shankly's old team Huddersfield Town when Billy was tasked with taking a penalty to put his side 3-2 ahead. He was looking to score his 35th Liverpool penalty and his mind was set on power, too much power. His penalty kick reverberated around Anfield as it walloped the crossbar with such power that the ball burst, the same ball that was almost knocking players out as often as it was being passed in this era. The cannon of a left foot had not gone, but maybe the eye for goal was diminishing.

The second memorable moment came in a match at home to Stoke City. Young Roger Hunt was making a name for himself in Shankly's resurgent side, lifted to third by the end of the season, and he scored the first in this 5-1 victory against Stoke. Hunt continued to impress, and when he crossed the ball five minutes before the break, it met the left foot of Liddell and for the final time he found the back of the net. Fittingly, the loss of the toss had meant that Liverpool were kicking to the Kop for the first half, so his final goal was scored in front of the ones who loved him dearest. The age of 38 years and 55 days meant that Billy was, and remains, the oldest player to ever score for Liverpool. A fitting tribute to his longevity.

The following seasons saw the first of Billy's three final matches for Liverpool. Of the 37,000 in attendance in August 1960, no one knew for sure whether it would be the final time he would represent the Liverpool first team. The appearance made him the oldest post-war player to play an outfield match for Liverpool. He was still to represent the club at reserve level but never again amongst the club's elite. The physique was still there, but little else was living up to the legacy that had so long graced Merseyside.

The upsetting report from the *Daily Express* read: 'Billy Liddell, the once-great footballer who is 39 in February, was thrown back into the furnace of League football last night in place of Liverpool centre-forward Dave Hickson. But though the heart is still in his great frame, the reflexes are gone. I winced every time Billy fumbled an attempt to trap, turn and shoot. And I say Liverpool must stop asking the impossible of a man who is still Anfield's idol.'

After a loss to Southampton, Billy's final match was in the Central League for the reserves at Anfield, captain Liddell assisting and scoring in a 5-0 victory in front of just over 2,000 supporters. When the match finished a few of the players put Billy on their shoulders and carried him off the pitch.

Billy's step down to the reserves, or 'stiffs' as they were often colloquially called, allowed a lot of the budding players an opportunity to witness the great man first-hand. He never displayed any upset or anger that he had been dropped, instead leading by example and speaking few but wise words like those uttered to Alan Banks: 'All the best, go and play your normal game.' This would have been a dream for the reserve team manager Joe Fagan, young lads playing alongside their childhood hero.

This era of wage caps, reserve, A, B and C teams meant that there was an abundance of Liverpool players in the squad. Billy was the eldest of around 55 men but never sulked that he was being displaced within the first team. Shankly would always welcome him to speak in training and he made sure his players listened to Billy: 'Listen to Billy lads, he's been there, he's done it all!'

* * *

There were two key reasons that Billy left Liverpool. The most obvious and understandable reason was that when his contract expired in May 1961 he was 39 years old. The other was financial. Glancing at a 1960 wage scale for the club shows that Billy was being paid £20 a week with the chance of a £2 bonus. His take-home pay was £16 2s. 11d., when his income tax, house rental and insurance had been deducted. Players being paid by the cloth bank bag full of half-crowns being passed around the dressing room is a further example of the monumental financial changes in football! Those days, £20 was the maximum wage, which Billy deserved to be a recipient of. However, when Shankly was battling with a cash-strapped board, he had to offload some big earners to build his new team. Nearly 40 and quickly deteriorating in talent, Billy was the obvious candidate for the chop.

There is no room for sentimentality in football. Shankly learned this the hard way during his own barren period. From 1966–73 Liverpool failed to win a trophy, and with his side in transition, Shankly remained too loyal to his Second Division conquering team. It was not until he broke up this band of brothers that he could bring further silverware, leaving the Reds in the perfect position for Bob Paisley's European and domestic trophy-hoarding red men to take over.

The combination of Liddell and Shankly was special. It saw two great Scots, ex-team-mates at Scotland and wartime Liverpool, and tremendously important people in the history of the club, come together. Similarities could certainly have been drawn to that of Steven Gerrard and Jürgen Klopp, had Gerrard remained with the club for one more season.

Despite the respect between the two Scots, it was Shankly who had to help end the aged Liverpool hero's career. Upon his arrival, Shankly needed results to win the supporters' trust. The 1961/62 season proved to be the campaign when Liverpool were finally promoted as champions. That season showcased Shankly's shrewd transfer market ability and management skills.

He highlighted a list of 24 names of players he wanted to leave the club inside a year of his arrival, believing the club was overburdened with too many substandard and overpaid players. One of the men on this list was club legend Billy Liddell. Although the decision may not have seemed too hard to make as Billy was now an elderly player, it was still difficult to replace a man of that stature within the club. Nevertheless, Shankly did so and he was firmly building his own team.

Shankly had frictions with the Liverpool board of directors. He described them as 'gamblers on a losing streak who were afraid to bet anymore'. This was largely due to the 13 years the club had been without a trophy, and the six years they had spent in the Second Division. Despite strong performances in Shankly's first two seasons, Liverpool had still not been promoted and the board was not confident enough to financially support all his plans.

This was until the arrival of Eric Sawyer, an ambitious man whose arrival gave Shankly the backing he needed at a higher level.

Shankly put two players at the top of his transfer wish list – Ron Yeats and Ian St John – but the board still met his desires with scepticism, stating that the club could not afford them. However, the newest member of the board of directors, Sawyer, spoke up and said, 'We cannot afford not to buy them.'

For Billy's replacement, Shankly was happy to look within the club. Together with his talented coaching staff that included Paisley, several young players were allowed the chance to impress. In all, there were five youngsters who were being tried: Billy Howard, Reggie Blore, Willie Carlin, Alan A'Court and the man who got the role, Ian Callaghan. This was before Kevin Lewis and Johnny Wheeler were brought in to challenge too.

Alan A'Court had come into the squad and was playing on the right, while Billy had been moved to centre-forward before Callaghan came into the side as a teen. The five young men did not realise the importance of the matches they were playing under Paisley in the youth teams at the time. Lewis, A'Court and Wheeler were the quick fix to the Liddell hole, but Callaghan became the permanent replacement.

The 'potentials' were all being tried at outside-right to take Billy's position and there could not be many better

Author, Peter Kenny Jones, on the Billy Liddell bench outside Anfield. (Picture by Warren Kane McCann). (Right) Author, Peter Kenny Jones, with Rob Storrey (OTK Flags) with the 'Liddellpool' flag at Anfield

Billy Liddell and the 1957/58 Liverpool squad
Courtesy of Michael Makison

Billy, Malcolm, and David Liddell. Courtesy of Rena Liddell

Billy Liddell and the Scotland national team. Courtesy of Rena Liddell

Billy Liddell with the RAF football team.
Courtesy of Rena Liddell

Back Row: Betty Liddell, Sheila Liddell
Second Row: George Liddell, Alastair
Liddell. Third Row: Phyllis Liddell, Billy
Liddell. Fourth Row: Marion Liddell,
Montgomery Liddell. Front Row: Malcolm
Liddell, Linda, Margaret, Rena Liddell,
David Liddell. Taken at the University
of Liverpool Guild of Students, Masonic
Dance.
Courtesy of Rena Liddell

Four generations of Liddell, Billy as a child.
Courtesy of Rena Liddell

Billy at David Liddell's wedding.
Courtesy of Rena Liddell

Billy Liddell in RAF uniform, navigator.
Courtesy of Rena Liddell

When Billy got his wings, taken
by Norvals photographers in
Dunfermline.
Courtesy of Rena Liddell

Billy and Rena Liddell, outside the Britannia, Liverpool.
Courtesy of Rena Liddell

Malcolm, Billy and David Liddell.
Courtesy of Rena Liddell

Malcolm, Billy, Phyllis, David Liddell.
Courtesy of Rena Liddell

Back Row: Alastair, Rena, George. Front Row: Phyllis, Malcolm, Billy, David, Montgomery
At Windsor Road, Tuebrook, Liverpool. Courtesy of Rena Liddell

David, Billy, Malcolm, Phyllis Liddell at Westfield Avenue, Broadgreen, Liverpool.
Courtesy of Rena Liddell

Billy and Phyllis Liddell
outside Westfield Avenue,
Broadgreen, Liverpool.
Courtesy of Rena Liddell

Back Row: Stephen, Jill. Front Row: Rena, Jemma, Anne, Rag, Phyllis,
Tom, David. At the unveiling of the Billy Liddell Memorial 2010.
Courtesy of Rena Liddell

Left to Right: Billy's friend, Rena, George, Betty, Alastair, Sheila, Phyllis, Billy, Norman Heavyside and son Ian. En route to Wembley' The bus was hired through the Liverpool University Guild of Students, where Billy worked after his football retirement.
Courtesy of Rena Liddell

Billy and Phyllis Liddell. St Andrew's Dinner.
Courtesy of Rena Liddell

George Telford (Best Man), Phyllis (Bride), Billy (Groom), Rena (Flower Girl), George (Page Boy). Billy's 40th wedding anniversary. Courtesy of Rena Liddell

Back Row: George, Alastair, Tom, Billy, Campbell. Front Row: Montgomery, Rena. The Liddells. Courtesy of Rena Liddell

made to replace Liddell than Callaghan, the man who would break Billy's appearance record with a similar level of respect in the game as a footballer and as a man. Billy's personal favourite as his successor was also Callaghan, something he passed on to his manager, Shankly. Callaghan was given his chance against Bristol Rovers in April 1960, his performance gathering headlines, and it was clear to everyone that the changing of the guard was in full motion.

Despite the search for the replacement of the man who had yet to leave the club, Billy again never made anyone feel uneasy about the fact that his end was being planned out. He appreciated all the club had done for him, wanted to serve them as long as they needed him and leave before he became a burden, while helping to inspire the young players primed to replace him.

* * *

The big day of Liddell appreciation came in September 1960, the first testimonial at Anfield for a former Red since Jackie Sheldon's testimonial in 1922. Close to 40,000 packed out Anfield on a wretched evening that followed a rain-soaked day.

Stanley Matthews scuppered the pre-match plans as he failed to attend the match. Johnny Wheeler was drafted in for Liverpool and Billy played for the all-star International XI, remaining selfless on a day that was all about him. Matthews had form for failing to attend charity matches and testimonials as he knew his name would help to sell tickets for the benefactor. He was seemingly happy to let everyone down at the last minute.

One winger who did respect his invitation was Tom Finney. The then-retired Prestonian turned Ronnie Moran inside out all match. Finney and Liddell soon swapped positions and it was Billy's turn to run riot out wide. Moran was still very much part of Shankly's side but was not expecting such a torrid time in an exhibition match. He received a large laugh when he turned to the fans and shrugged his shoulders after being beaten by Finney and Liddell for the umpteenth time that night.

Billy led both sides out to a fantastic reception as the Clan McLeod Pipe Band performed some traditional Scottish music before the match. No sooner had bagpipes been packed than Billy had scored. He put Liverpool behind by scoring in his favoured Kop end goal. Liverpool keeper Bert Slater was continually booed for his efforts to stop Billy from adding to his tally. Dave Hickson and Alan A'Court helped Liverpool notch four goals before Slater remained the villain as he refused to let Billy see out the match with another goal. Despite the referee playing a further six minutes to cap off the performance, proceedings had to be brought to an end without a Liddell second.

The crowd remained packed into the sodden stadium as they anticipated Billy's speech over the tannoy. No sooner had the match finished, hands been shaken and the sweat wiped from his brow, than Billy jogged over to give his final speech to his fans:

> This evening has been a greater ordeal for me than playing in the Cup Final. But I want to thank all the stars who came along to help me and also my team-mates for putting up such a grand show. I want to tell all you Liverpool supporters what a wonderful thing it has been to have your support.
>
> I would ask that you show the same enthusiasm to the rest of the team as you have done for me. If you do that, we can put Liverpool back where we belong, in the First Division. Thank you all very much, you're the best in the world!

The rarely seen emotional Liddell was tearing up as he finished his short but sweet speech to his adoring fans. The players formed a guard of honour as he waved to all four sides of the ground and left the pitch for a final time. The match was also emotional for the supporters in attendance, many tears being wiped as the father of Liverpool football left them with a real feeling of a loss of a family member and friend whom many had grown up with.

A testimonial is now often played in support of a charity that the player would like their supporters to donate to. In this era, the testimonial would help set the player up for retirement and was a huge honour. This match bought Billy a new home, and the £6,340 received from ticket sales was the equivalent of over six years' wages. The appreciation of his years of service tangibly stood in Chequers Gardens in the leafy suburb of Aigburth.

The *Liverpool Echo* produced a giant souvenir edition paper of Billy's career highlights as a thank you for his services to Merseyside football. Billy received a leather-bound copy of the paper, which he proudly kept as a keepsake. The front page reads:

> Billy Liddell, the city salutes you as a player, a gentleman, a sportsman and the finest clubman the game ever knew. The plaudits at Anfield tonight will come from Liverpudlian and Evertonian alike. They share affection for you as one of the few immortals of the game, one whose deeds and courage will be talked about for generations. This may not be your last game, but it is the one which will mark, officially, your impending retirement from the sport you have adorned. It will leave you in no doubt about the regard in which you are held.

Liverpool went on to achieve the riches Billy would never have even thought possible for his Liverpool team to have dreamed of. Shankly was no doubt the catalyst. In fact, try to pick any combination of superlatives to attempt to describe his importance to the club. It is both fitting and upsetting that Billy's legacy could spill all the way over to Bill Shankly's boys, but painfully unlucky how close he was to the future success of the club.

It perhaps would have been more fitting for Billy to reach the round figure of 40 and score a crucial goal or play in one last important match that helped Liverpool return to the top. As this chapter stated at the start though, there is no place for sentiment in competitive football.

The send-off Liddellpool received was as much for the fans as it was for Billy. They were all waving goodbye to the man who had defined the club in its most painful playing era. The emotional goodbye from Billy was so unassuming, yet it showed to everyone how much the club meant to him and how happy he was to hand it over to the next great custodian. Liddellpool no more – it was time for Liverpool to stand alone and be reborn.

The Men Who Put the Pool into Liddellpool – Jimmy Melia

Jimmy Melia – Liverpool FC (1953–1964)

He was amongst the best five players that have ever played for Liverpool. Two-footed player, terrific in the air, two great feet, right foot and left foot, and he was that good at Liverpool they called them Liddellpool.

I played with him for about six years. He never had a lot of players to play with in them days as the club and the team weren't very good, but he was very loyal to Liverpool. He could score goals with his right foot, his left foot, his head; he could play on the wing, he could play centre-forward, could play anywhere and, more importantly, he would be a starter in the modern Liverpool team today, that's how good he was. When I first went there, he took all the corners, all the free kicks, all the penalties, he was captain.

One week he wasn't playing at Swansea, so we needed someone to take the penalties and so the manager said, 'Who wants to take the penalties?' Phil Taylor was the manager then, so I said, 'I'll take it boss.' I scored the penalty at Swansea. So, the next game we were playing Bristol Rovers at home and we were walking out on to the field and Phil Taylor said, 'Jimmy, if there's a penalty, you take it.' Billy was back in the team, so we get out there and 15 minutes into the game we get a penalty, so I pick the ball up. All the crowd booed me because Billy wasn't taking the penalty! I put it down on the spot, and I put it in the back of the net and they still booed me! That's just because Billy didn't take the penalty. I don't know what they would have done if I had missed!

I played my first game, and he gave me my first goal, the first goal I ever scored for the club, which was in front of the Kop. It was a cross from Billy on the left-hand side and I met the ball and put it in the back of the net. I went to the club at 15 years old and I worked on the ground staff, so we used to give out their uniforms, all their kit and everything else and join in with the second or third team, whichever we had the opportunity. If he ever spoke to me, I would go home and say, 'Billy Liddell spoke to me today!'

I would be nervous round him; he was Sir Billy, he was terrific. Same for any prospective player all over the country would be the same. He would always give you plenty of encouragement and whatever we needed. He would say, 'Go out there and enjoy yourself,' and tell us what to do, get out and just play your game.

I always remember him coming back to the club after he had finished playing. He would turn up, say hello and speak to people. It would be Anfield in the dressing room because he was a big friend of Paisley and, both being Scotsmen, him and Shankly knew each other from their playing days. He would speak with everyone, say hello, how are things going and wanting to know how everyone was. He was a perfect man all round.

I think he's unfortunate that today people don't really remember Billy Liddell like they should, in my opinion. The guy was a terrific player, up there with the best players to ever play for the club. Like Paisley, he did a hell of a job for the club.

One of the greatest players that ever played for Liverpool, one of the most genuine people, gave everything, strong as a bull, had all the ability in the world and that is why he scored so many goals.

10

Life After Football

FOOTBALLERS' LIVES typically become less hectic and less interesting, particularly in the eyes of the supporters, once they retire. Billy went from the King of the Kop to full-time accountant, all while juggling his Justice of the Peace (JP), church, Sunday school, freemasonry, writing, and any other pastime commitments that he had lined up. Although this was not as appreciated as playing in front of 50,000 spectators every week, it shows how Billy filled his time after retirement.

It is often seen that in the life of a footballer, the 20-odd-year career is spoken about at great length and then the remaining 40, 50, 60 years are glossed over in a few sentences. Billy's post-football retirement days were certainly jam-packed and deserve attention. Not just to extend the story of his fantastic life, but for sheer interest in the stories that can be told.

The formal end of Billy's Liverpool FC connections could have been extended if the club had been more accommodating, but he still managed to fit in more football-related appearances as well as a lengthy working career. Another major event would be his battle with dementia and the end of his life. Billy Liddell will forever be best remembered as a footballer, but the 40 years that followed his Anfield departure will show that he was much more than just that.

* * *

Beginning with football, Billy wanted to remain fit and active but there was no formal continuation with the game after his retirement. However, there were several incidents when his footballing status provided him with opportunities to dip his toe back in.

The main way that Billy maintained a relationship with football was through testimonial and charity matches. While real competitive edge was not present, this showed how revered he was due to the calibre of players that requested his presence. To quickly name a few that Billy played in: Frank Phillips of Prescot Cables in 1959, Tom Finney of Preston North End in 1960, Nat Lofthouse of Bolton Wanderers in 1958. Although he did not play in Gerry Byrne's testimonial in 1970, due to the success of his own testimonial he provided a lot of help in convincing players to partake – even Stanley Matthews said yes! However, Billy did take part in a five-a-side match at half-time alongside Bill Shankly, Bob Paisley, Joe Fagan, Reuben Bennett, Tony

Waiters, Ronnie Moran, Geoff Twentyman, Jimmy Tarbuck and Stuart Hall.

During Nat Lofthouse's testimonial, in what was another horrendously rainy evening, Billy delighted supporters with his performance. He hit a shot from 25 yards that struck the crossbar so venomously that supporters claimed it quaked for nearly a minute, as the rain fell from the saturated bar.

The main charity match that will be remembered from Billy's retirement football appearances would be the Ferenc Puskás XI vs Billy Liddell XI in May 1967. South Liverpool FC, an amateur team in Liverpool, agreed to host a charity match to raise money for charitable causes in the area and took to attracting some famous football names. Billy, being so involved in charity work, was first port of call to captain a side and help attract some recently retired players.

To draw in the crowds, attention was turned to a marquee foreign name. Pelé was approached but was too busy with his Brazilian club, Santos. The brazen selection committee chanced sending a request to the 40-year-old Puskás, who was still playing for Real Madrid. Remarkably, the Hungarian agreed to play, and news spread like wildfire.

Billy met Puskás, the 'Galloping Major' as he was known, at Liverpool airport before some public appearances in support of the charities that the match proceeds would go towards. Over 10,000 supporters crammed into the stadium to witness a true great of the game … play against Puskás!

Billy's side ran out 5-3 victors on a day when players such as John Charles, Dave Hickson, Billy Bingham and Malcolm Allison turned out to help raise money for the local area. The match was a huge success for local charities and has been immortalised in Liverpool South Parkway train station, where a plaque commemorates the event, the station now standing where the stadium was on that day.

Billy's relationship with Liverpool FC was all but cut following his contract expiration in 1961. Following his testimonial, the fans had wanted to permanently honour his legacy within Anfield. During the annual board of directors meeting in 1964, it was discussed that there had been a clamour from the supporters for the Kemlyn Road Stand at Anfield to be renamed. The overwhelming majority wanted it to be known as the 'Billy Liddell Stand'. This decision was indefinitely shelved and never came to fruition.

There are only four stands to a football stadium and it is a lot easier to name one after a player than it is to take the name away. The board may have felt that it was not right to name the stand after Billy so early in the club's history, this being just over 70 years since its inception. Only one man, Sir Kenny Dalglish, has a stand in his honour at Anfield, which proves two things: one, Dalglish is thought of in incredibly high esteem by all involved in the club; and two, the club has a history of not wanting to name stands after players.

This can be viewed as right or wrong and, as mentioned, there are only four stands, so if the club had the Elisha Scott

Stand, Billy Liddell Stand, Bob Paisley Stand and the Bill Shankly Stand, what would they have done to honour Kenny Dalglish and perhaps Steven Gerrard? It is a tough balance and Liverpool have established a good way of remembering the important figures within the club through statues, gates, plaques and benches around the stadium.

However, the club should have listened to the supporters in 1964 and found a way of honouring Billy, whether through renaming a stand or whatever other method they came up with. There are too many examples in football and in life of posthumous appreciation for significant individuals who should have been celebrated when they were alive. Maybe in contradiction to writing a book and celebrating the 100th birthday of a man who is no longer alive, too much is done after people die, which could have been done when they were able to witness it first-hand.

The Shankly and Paisley gates and statues at Anfield are a great tribute to the importance of two of the most significant men in Liverpool's illustrious history. However, Bill and Bob would certainly have preferred to have been able to see them built before they died.

Billy Liddell is a name that sits alongside Elisha Scott, Bill Shankly, Bob Paisley, Kenny Dalglish, John Barnes and Steven Gerrard as the men honoured and immortalised with benches outside the ground. The omission of people such as Ian Rush, Ian Callaghan, Ronnie Moran, Alex Raisbeck, Ron Yeats – the list could go on and on – shows how highly thought of Billy is in Liverpool's history. The inclusion of Dalglish, Barnes and Gerrard also shows that the club is getting better at honouring important people and players while they are alive to receive the adulation of their supporters. The choice of Sammy Lee and Rafa Benítez to work for the blue side of Merseyside may also show why sometimes it is best to wait before honouring some!

Kenny Dalglish has been able to enjoy his legacy in a way that Shankly, Paisley and Liddell never could. That is unfortunate for Billy as he should have been able to visit Anfield after his retirement and see a permanent reminder of his importance to the club and the fans. Instead, it is only his family, friends and supporters who will now be able to see his bench, the plaque in the club museum and the Liddellpool flag on the Kop and feel a similar sense of pride in his importance to Liverpool.

The board illustrated how out of touch they were with the fans and failed to honour Billy correctly in 1964 and during the rest of his lifetime. This is despite the fact he had been the man who was keeping them in the Second Division, keeping fans wanting to come to watch Liverpool, and who sacrificed so much of his life to serve them. Posthumous honour always feels too little, too late. Billy and many other great players have never been able to get the true thanks they deserved.

Although this decision would not have upset Billy, if he ever even knew about it being discussed, another decision in 1971 certainly did. The 62-year-old Merseyside company director and head of the Liverpool and Bootle Police Authority, Alderman Arthur Collins, resigned as a member of the board of directors at Liverpool. Billy put his name forward for the role, alongside four others.

One of the prerequisites for an application to become a director was to obtain shares in the club. Following the death of James Hampson, a former shareholder and Liverpool supporter, Billy was left shares within the will. This again exemplifies the magnitude of Billy Liddell – that he was given these from a fan in a will – but it also meant that he could now attend annual shareholders' meetings and apply for the position of director.

The current manager of the time was Billy's last, Bill Shankly, and he had said, 'It's no easy task being a director, especially if I'm the manager.' His Liverpool legacy, intelligence and business aptitude would surely have made Billy the perfect candidate for the role. Instead, the fruit merchant wholesaler Jack Cross won the vote, the 58-year-old inexplicably pipping Billy to a job he desired and deserved. Having the ability to financially support the club as a board member was also key and it is likely Cross was much wealthier than Liddell, presumably influencing the decision made.

This would have been a great PR move, if nothing else, for Liverpool. Their former hero now on the board would make perfect sense, notwithstanding the fact that

Billy had great business and financial talents. This is like the efforts Shankly made to join the board after his retirement, but he was also batted away by those in charge. It seemed a deliberate act to show players, managers and fans that the board was an exclusive club that they did not want any interference with. The board thought it was above the club and had little regard to the opinions of supporters. For Liddell and Shankly it was a crushing blow and left them with a bitter taste in their mouths, feeling unwanted and embarrassed, so neither applied to join the board or any employment role through Liverpool FC again.

Despite this disappointment, Billy remained a fervent Liverpool supporter. He attended matches regularly at a time when the fortunes of the club were turned upside down. He never viewed this as a missed opportunity or with resentment, he just enjoyed going to watch his team play and win. Fans would be able to see him park his car in the Sandon car park and walk up to the match. Whenever he took his seat in the Main Stand he would be greeted with a cheer, particularly in the years immediately after his retirement. It was part of the pre-match routine, taking his seat around five minutes before kick-off, hearing his name being shouted before performing a small, embarrassed wave that received rapturous applause. One example of this came in 1965 before the match against Inter Milan, his pre-match wave to a raucous Kop raising the atmosphere to fever pitch. Then he would ensure every autograph was signed before leaving, frustrating Phyllis by how long it would take him.

The two would have a meal on each matchday in the sponsors' lounge and Billy would converse with players past and present. He always had time for the fans and young players if they ever wanted any advice or just a general chat, his favourite player becoming Ian Callaghan. In addition, Scots were always people he made a real effort with at Anfield, particularly Alan Hansen and Kenny Dalglish. For those who had watched him play, the opportunity to see him at the ground every matchday was like seeing an old family friend. Although he was not on the pitch sharing the medals and successes, he was enjoying them with his supporters around him.

Billy would also enjoy trips to Wembley, or Anfield South as it was coined for the vast number of times Liverpool travelled down south for a cup final. The opportunity to get up close with the current players meant that he could often visit the dressing room and get a picture with whichever trophy they had won that day. One of these visits also meant that he appeared on ITV's *Saint and Greavsie* with Ian St John and Jimmy Greaves.

Billy's connection to the football club and boys' clubs meant that he would often be in attendance for cup finals hosted at Anfield. This would not be solely Liverpool FC Boys but for the Liverpool area, teams such as Sefton Boys and Wirral Boys. He would attend the matches and hand out medals and the trophy at full time.

Preceding the 1977 Scotland vs Wales match, played at Anfield, Billy was part of a pre-match chat in the famous Boot Room at Anfield. Alongside him in the room was Ronnie Moran, his son Paul Moran, Joe Fagan, Bob Paisley, Jock Stein and Bill Shankly. Billy was amongst the elite in football as a peer, so respected by so many people and especially those with Liverpool and Scotland connections.

Throughout the 1970s and 1980s, while Liverpool were collecting silverware for fun, Billy had a lot of meet and greet events with Liverpool supporters' clubs. There would often be the opportunity to see that latest piece of silverware and meet Billy Liddell, shaking his hand and getting a picture with the cup.

April 1994 provided Billy an opportunity to receive a thank you from his adoring fans. Despite this occurring during a period of his life when he was fully feeling the effects of dementia, it is great that this occasion presented itself. Liverpool faced Norwich City on a day known as 'The Kop's Last Stand', the last match at Anfield before the all-standing Kop became fitted with seats. Prior to kick-off, the 44,000 supporters in attendance were introduced to Kenny Dalglish, Albert Stubbins, Ian Callaghan, Tommy Smith, Steve Heighway, David Johnson, Phil Thompson, David Fairclough, Craig Johnston, Joe Fagan, Nessie Shankly, Jessie Paisley and Billy Liddell. The ground was buzzing with nostalgia and appreciation for some of the former greats who had graced the Anfield turf.

On a day when the ground was full hours before kick-off, the chance for some of the Anfield faithful to honour their former heroes was taken by all in attendance. What this also provided was the first time that Billy Liddell's name was truly sung in full voice on the Kop. There had been the old banjo, nickelodeon and 'Give it to Billy' chants before, but not to the extent that his name was sung that day. The simple yet evocative 'There's only one Billy Liddell' greeted the Scot as he stepped foot on the pitch. Now in his seventies, Billy was able to fully see and feel the appreciation of a full Anfield for the first time in 30 years.

Phyllis had been worried that Billy would not be up for the event, particularly due to the fact he was to walk on to the pitch alone, and he nearly did not attend due to his health. However, the assurances of the club that he would be looked after eased her worries. Billy walked up the Anfield steps one final time and jogged across the turf he had graced so often before. Tommy Smith was then on hand to look after him, keeping hold of him and standing by his side until the families were able to join the ex-players on the pitch.

Although painfully sad that Billy certainly would not have had the opportunity to fully appreciate the magnitude of the situation, the kindness of the club, Tommy Smith and all the supporters ensured that it was an unforgettable moment of appreciation for Billy Liddell's role for Liverpool.

* * *

Retirement from football normally means a lot more free time – not for Billy Liddell. In the words of David, 'He seemed as busy as he always was with his other interests.' He merely swapped his two days' football training for two days of work with Simon Jude and West. Instead of playing for Liverpool, he would now go to watch them.

Wanting to keep his physical fitness meant that Billy played a lot more tennis. Holidays in Devon with the family would consist of competitive games of tennis between Billy and his sons, who were now in their twenties. Billy's love for tennis also saw him visit Wimbledon most years. This would be alongside pitch and putt that would see the three men spending time together after Billy's retirement. He also enjoyed playing snooker, squash and badminton in Liverpool University. He would later refuse to play against his sons as they started beating him too often!

Playing football was not off the agenda and he played with his colleagues from his role as a JP. However, Malcolm had to pick him up one evening and take him to hospital following a collision that saw Billy break his collarbone. Injury was a big part of post-retirement football for Billy as his body was getting weaker, the opposition getting younger and he was targeted for being such a great footballer. People wanted to go in hard and say they had tackled Billy Liddell.

There were rumours that Tranmere Rovers had asked whether Billy would be interested in taking the role of manager, but this was not something of interest to him. His mild manner and the lack of job security of a manager meant that he wanted to remain in office work. His working life soon saw him move to Liverpool University in 1962, where he was the assistant bursar to the guild of undergraduates. Phyllis also worked in the offices of the university and he got his sister Rena a job in salaries there.

Billy served his adopted city as a magistrate for 30 years and for the same length of time he was involved with the YMCA, the Merseyside Boys' Clubs and Merseyside Youth Association. Then there were the years of dedication to his church as a Sunday school teacher and treasurer, as well as his own youth club. He would also travel around churches and schools in Merseyside providing talks on football and his faith, spreading the word of God. During his visits to schools, the talks Billy gave would attract huge numbers. Classes that had only entertained around 15 students were soon bombarded by those old enough to have been able to see him play.

Billy had jobs, hobbies and pastimes galore and he was still avidly involved in his Scottish dancing with all the Liddell family. Alder Hey Children's Hospital and the Women's Voluntary Service were graced with his work as a disc jockey for them. The Littlewood's pools forecast was another in a long list.

Perhaps most well-known was his role as a JP. Phyllis was so delighted when he was appointed, as she saw it as better than being a footballer! He was one of the first players to become a JP while still playing football, filling his time with more unselfish work for his community. The role entailed hearing cases in court and contributing to decision-making on more minor legal issues.

Ironically, Billy was a winger as a JP. There are three JPs, also called magistrates, with a Presiding Justice and two wingers. The wingers would have the same responsibility and role as the Presiding Justice, other than they would have to speak to the court. Billy often held the role of winger on and off the field! During his time as a magistrate, supporters would be in awe of a man helping to convict them of a crime or issue a fine. Some supporters even asked for Billy's signature after they had been found guilty! One such example of this is Liverpool comedian Billy Shine:

> I got a speeding fine and I had to go to court. I heard that Billy could be on the bench, so I had a Liverpool top on. Would you believe he still done me! It was a red T-shirt with the Liverpool logo in the corner. He definitely saw what it was and he just sat there and let them say 'five pounds', and I was trying to shove my red shirt towards him, but no, the miserable old man should have let me off!

Billy's second retirement came when he left Liverpool University after 30 years' service. The introduction of computers and the fact he was now in his 60s prompted his decision to retire. His work was largely alongside students and many had become unaware or disinterested in his former life as a footballer. However, the odd historically versed Liverpool supporter would recognise and have the honour of working alongside him. One such supporter and student was Dominic Myers, who recalled Billy's retirement from the role in 1984:

> I was well aware that the Guild of Undergraduates was very fortunate to have the legendary Liverpool striker Mr Billy Liddell as the Bursar, but most students were neither interested in student politics nor barely knew the Guild office existed, so very few even knew they had the opportunity to meet the iconic Red. But if you tried to engage with Billy on his 228 goals or his exploits and memories as a Liverpool and Scotland player, he was so modest. If you asked Billy for a prediction for the weekend's game he would say, 'They are doing quite well, I think they will win,' so typically under-spoken, gentle and not wanting to bring the attention to his glory.
>
> Billy was always so neat and tidy and always precise in his work. It seemed disrespectful of such a

legend to call him Billy, so he was always Mr Liddell. Billy just did his work quietly, arrived on time and left on time. I gradually got to know Billy a bit better but, of course, he was always completely neutral in his opinions with regard to any of the student issues and political views. As twenty-somethings working alongside a retiring 'civil servant' we did feel he was a little slow and conservative in his movements.

I remember that afternoon when we presented the cake to him to appreciate his service and wish him a happy retirement. We had invited all of the student officers, Guild Council [representatives from the student body] and the University Senate to the retirement event but I remember I was sad and disappointed by the poor turnout. Most of them were not interested and had very little appreciation of his career with Liverpool or the years at the university, which was a longer period than most of us were old! I gave a short speech, can't remember what I said, but I know I was so proud to have worked alongside him. My time as President was a special part of my life and the time with Billy a relatively minor part of that but disproportionately important to me.

Although those present were not as appreciative as they should have been towards a man who had dedicated so much of his life to them, the city and one of its football teams,

Billy enjoyed his time in the university and it was a big part of his post-football life.

Clearly an intelligent man, Billy was not just a footballer. There have not been too many footballers with the ability or opportunity to show both intellect and football prowess. Maybe Brian Hall and Steve Heighway were other exceptions to the rule at Liverpool, but Billy certainly was with his post-retirement working life.

Religion also remained of vital importance to Billy throughout his retirement. Such was his religious belief and adoration amongst the fans that it was said that if Billy were Catholic, he could have been the Pope! His faith and attendance at Methodist Church meant a lot to him. He would talk about Ireland with Rena and how he thought the violence between north and south was 'very silly'. His religion was of paramount importance, but never something he wanted to fight about or preach about to people.

* * *

Phyllis was very private over Billy's illness, so not much was known about his health in the latter years of his life. It appears that signs of difficulty remembering and processing events was evident during the Hillsborough disaster in 1989. Billy did not seem to be able to grasp what had happened, so the family became worried about his behaviour. He just sat down and started reading the programme while the disaster was unfolding in front of him.

The start of his struggles with memory dated back to the 1970s, and by 1994 at Anfield, the condition was severe enough that the club needed to provide Billy with help, but he was well enough to run on to the pitch unaided. The family was immensely proud that Billy could be part of that day and do so without demonstrating any major side effects. Phyllis stood by him continuously during his illness. She did not want anyone other than close friends and family to know about his health.

A common symptom of dementia is being stuck in the past, and it does seem that the opportunity for Billy's ex-team-mates to come to see him and reminisce would have been helpful. However, Phyllis would have been the person with the best knowledge and understanding of his condition, and she wanted it to be kept within the family, so that is what happened. Because of this bond they had, Billy would rely more and more on his wife, visibly distressed when she was not by his side.

Billy would become interested in different pastimes, such as gardening, and his behaviour was changing very quickly. His twins had left the family home and they were noticing how hard it was to get conversation out of him. The decline was slow but still very upsetting, meaning that Phyllis had to move Billy into a home to support her care for him.

He would still love to spend time with children, and the young members of the family would keep Billy entertained with games of hide and seek. He would show them his football books and memorabilia and their visits would really cheer him up. He would still watch the football, even when his illness was at its very worst and he had become less verbal. While sitting in his chair and watching the match, his legs would kick the ball.

Billy's famous 19-inch neck withered away and he was now frail and weighing less than ten stone. Occasionally, football memories would get him talking but for the majority of the time he was quiet and vacant. In fact, if it had not been for the pacemaker that had been fitted, he would have died much earlier.

This was no quick health battle that killed Billy; he lived with it for over 20 years. He was a family man and would still be able to leave the care home, but he was becoming progressively confused. Calls to his sons, who had left home, would be quiet, and when they visited him, he would tell the same stories or show them the same newspaper article multiple times. Weekly family visits and talking about the past would see an improvement in his condition but he became increasingly quiet and reclusive.

It has been mentioned as much as possible the links between the head injuries that Billy suffered and the probable links to dementia. He is not the only footballer to have died after being diagnosed with the disease – men such as Bob Paisley, Brian Clough, Jack Charlton and Jeff Astle are among some of the most well-known. It does not need to be discussed again here, but there needs to be more accountability in football for the obvious link between head injuries, the use of heavy leather footballs and dementia.

It seems so cruel that a man of Billy's stature, who had achieved so much in his life, had it all stripped away by dementia. His memories had gone and he had a very cruel end to his life, without the opportunity to thoroughly enjoy a long and happy retirement with his wife. It became inevitable that his life was nearing an end and the family just had to wait for the illness to kill him. Billy had been so rich in memories and success but died poor at the hands of the disease.

* * *

The legacy of Billy Liddell will remain much longer than he did, but all stories have an ending. After a long battle with dementia, Billy died in his Mossley Hill nursing home on 3 July 2001, aged 79. It was expected after his deteriorating health and in many ways came as a blessing because he was a shadow of the man he once was. His death occurred in a week that also saw the deaths of former Liverpool manager Joe Fagan and director Tom Saunders.

Billy's death certificate denoted that he died of old age, which was something Phyllis was happy about as she did not want him to be known as someone who died of this terrible illness. Despite this, and not wanting to cause offence to anyone within the family, there must be a time when his death is discussed, particularly the causes of it.

This is such an important topic that needs to be discussed and tackled head on.

His funeral was held at his church, Court Hey Methodist Church in Huyton, and relayed to the large crowds of people outside before the funeral procession moved to Springwood Crematorium in Allerton, on 9 July. 'How Great Thou Art' and 'Amazing Grace' were sung, alongside a reading of 'The Lord is My Shepherd', with donations being sent to the NSPCC. There was then a wake in Woolton where some ex-players joined the family in celebrating Billy's life and their memories of him.

The vast crowds present were emblazoned in red and white as they paid tribute to their hero. Fans travelled from around the world to come to say thank you to a man who had given them so much happiness during his life.

The news of Billy's death was obviously sad, but somewhat of a blessing for the family as they knew the poor quality of life he was enduring and the toll this was taking on Phyllis. However, for the fans, who were largely unaware of his condition or how severe it was, many were devastated. News of his illness spread following altercations with a confused Billy and worries about his lack of public appearances. People were aware he was ill and that the time would be soon, that they would find out he had died, then phoning each other and passing on the news, sharing memories of what Billy had meant to them before making the pilgrimage from near and far to pay their respects.

Tributes were also paid in the media, too many to mention. Billy's face was on every news bulletin and in most newspapers, such was his impact on football. *The Mirror* wrote: 'Even though he never made any money from the game, Liddell will always be remembered by Liverpool fans as one of their all-time greats, a star bigger than any of today's rich and famous players.'

Billy's busy retirement was crammed with lots of working and happy memories. The Liverpool directors' rejection and then the sorrowful battle with dementia were certainly not what he and the Liddell family deserved for the end of his life. They could all rejoice in the legacy he had at Liverpool, and the Kop singing his name during its last stand in 1994 was a fitting tribute to a man just seven years from his death. The funeral provided everyone an opportunity to mourn their hero, Billy Liddell, who had in truth left them many years before.

The Men Who Put the Pool into Liddellpool – Billy Howard

Billy Howard – Liverpool FC (1956–1962)

My first memory at about five years old was sitting on a crush barrier with my dad facing our left wing as we looked on from the Kop. I don't remember much apart from my dad and other fans talking about him. The view from the Kop was about 20 steps up, which was a great view as we attacked the Kop and watching Billy run down the wing and crossing such inviting balls for our forwards. It was a great view when Billy was taking corners.

As I got older and could understand the game more, Billy obviously became one of my football heroes. He was so focused on what his role was in the team, a model sportsman who never seemed ruffled, he accepted the laws of the game and was a credit to his profession.

It always amazed me that he was a part-time player, which his fitness belied. He was always equal to the task. I remember being on the top deck of a bus coming up from town and we lived off Crown Street; the bus stopped outside Liverpool University to pick up passengers. I looked to my left and was taken aback, looking through a window there was Billy sitting at his desk. I later found out he was a bursar at Liverpool University. This became a regular journey for me. I would walk down to the Adelphi and get a bus back, just to look through that window in the hope of seeing Billy, who was my hero by then. I must say it was only a penny in those days, but this journey came to an end when we moved up to Everton and went to live close to Anfield stadium at the top of Mere Lane, Heyworth Street. I changed schools then and soon after I was lucky enough to train and play some games with Liverpool schoolboys. I became a keen autograph hunter by then and I learned that Billy and his family had opened a shop on Walton Breck Road, so it wasn't long before I was a regular visitor to that shop! Not to buy anything but just in the hope that I would see Billy and get him to sign the many pictures in my scrapbooks.

Billy started to recognise me instantly as one of the boys that would be waiting for autographs before and after home games at Anfield. He asked me one day while he was signing my pics, 'Will you pass the word around to the other autograph hunters that if you get to the ground one hour before report time I will sign all pics, books, programmes. etc. But would you inform them not to ask after matches so I can get home to my family?' Of course, I was happy to pass on that request for my hero and amazingly everyone complied. All the lads were happy to do this such was the esteem he was held in, but he earned this respect by his own example.

At the age of 14 I found myself at Melwood. A scout had recommended me and here I am. I was to stay for six years, although for the last three I struggled with my ankle injury and had to tell the staff and they thought my ankle wouldn't stand up to the demands at the top level. Although I was a player with LFC, I still collected autographs until I was about 17 years old because it felt strange to ask mates for autographs after games and training at Melwood; it was a bit embarrassing really.

I still called into Billy's shop. If he was not yet home his wife would tell me when he was expected and to wait if I wanted; a couple of times she gave me a cup of tea. He would ask me if I played for the school and told me practice was important. 'Practise, practise.' That's all he ever said to me. I never did tell him that I got to Melwood because it was a bit embarrassing for me. It was a huge blow when Billy's career came to an end. I was at his testimonial and can still remember when Stanley Matthews's telegram was read out of the tannoy at the match. I can still remember the words: 'Sorry Billy, I am indisposed.'

In my view, Billy was the finest player ever to play for LFC from my time watching from 1946/47 until the present day. He was the one constant that kept LFC at the forefront of English football all through our lean times in the 1950s. It could be said he was a one-man team.

It was pleasing to know he was still about the place on matchdays. Men and women of my age group still talk fondly of Billy and his memory will never die. Billy was also a JP and he kept a lot of youngsters on the straight and narrow. I remember a mother telling me that her son had been up before Billy at one time, and afterwards Billy would come to his home to see how he was doing and how he could help keep him on the straight and narrow. That's the kind of man he was. If it was a player, a fan, a man in the street, or even an Everton fan, you could not help but admire this man. Not only as a footballer but as a real gentleman. He was a credit to the game.

When the news came that Billy was ill, a friend of mine, boxer Johnny Cook, told me he was going to visit Billy at home with Liverpool comedian Stevie Faye and asked me if I would like to join them. Apart from not wanting to encroach on the family space and knowing that they would probably be inundated with people wanting to say their goodbyes, I couldn't bring myself to go. That broke my heart but I just couldn't go, much as I wanted to, because I just didn't want to see Billy like that.

My love for LFC had started with him. My love for the game had started with him. So, when Johnny Cook had told me he was struggling I just didn't want to burden him. I would sit in the dressing room at Melwood and Anfield and all the time I would wonder how I got to be a part of my boyhood club with my hero Billy. If I had never kicked another football again, just to have walked around and played where my all-time hero had walked before me, what an absolute privilege and an honour to have been a small part of the same club. So small as to be insignificant really, but significant all the same. I was blessed, blessed to have met Billy.

Epilogue – Thanks Billy

THE FLYING SCOTSMAN

An old man wipes away a tear
and recollects a time
when he watched a flying Scotsman
weave his magic down the line

And from the line this legend
would then dance into the middle
he'd then unleash a thunderbolt
as the crowd sang, 'Billy Liddell'

He left his home in Perthshire
in the summer of thirty eight
but war broke out and intervened
before his name was great

An RAF navigator
was his role in World War Two
and with Sir Matt and Shankly
he was capped in forty two

When the war was over
he sure made up for lost time
as Liverpool's leading scorer
in eight seasons out of nine

'Give it to Billy, give it to Billy'
was the song the Kopites roared
as he sent them into ecstasy
with every goal he scored

Football then unlike today
wasn't laced with gold
you had to find another job
to provide when you got old

His intelligence and integrity
would stand him in good stead
he was Bursar, accountant and JP
as well as a famous red

He represented Great Britain
in forty seven and fifty five
with the great Sir Stanley Matthews
together by his side

His appearances for Liverpool
totalled 537
with 229 goal returns
a proud record to take to heaven

The fifties was a decade
when rock 'n' roll emerged
he was a rock who rolled defenders
while down the wing he surged

My old man always told me
when I was still at school
about this brilliant legend
who they nicknamed 'Liddellpool'

But despite his hero status
his ego never waved
one of life's true gentlemen
impeccably behaved

He genuinely adored the fans
and always gave his time
he'd stay behind for hours
till all autographs were signed

EPILOGUE – THANKS BILLY

His final days of stardom
were to start another phase
He stepped down for 'Sir Roger'
at the start of Shankly's days

A testimonial followed
beneath the Anfield skies
where to this flying Scotsman
forty thousand said goodbye

The years went by and he grew old
with dignity and pride
his family Christian values
and wife Phyllis by his side

How sad it was to hear about
his lonely mental state
the same disease that struck 'Sir Bob'
had struck this all-time great

As the decades come and go
many legends we have known
Hunt, St John, Keegan, Dalglish,
Rush, Fowler, Owen

263

So many gifted players
who did wonders with a ball
and William Beveridge Liddell
is right up there with them all

The old man who was weeping
wipes away another tear
that old man is my father
who's adored him all these years

I never got to see him play
I never had the pleasure
God bless you Bill from one old man
for the memories he treasures

[Words by Dave Kirby, Writer – 2001]

Although Billy's life met its end in 2001, this book is testament that his legacy has continued. He was a great footballer who cared about his family, a staunch professional, charitable man and legend of the club. Had he been alive today, his records would have been even more appreciated as he would not have had a huge gap during wartime football and would have had more fixtures to compete in domestically and in Europe.

He created his legacy as a terrific footballer who may not have won many trophies, but his loyalty, ability and longevity all helped ensure that he will forever be part of Liverpool folklore. As has been mentioned, his life has been posthumously celebrated at Anfield through the plaque in the museum, unveiled by Phyllis and Ian Callaghan in 2004, which reads:

> The great 'Billy' joined Liverpool from Scottish junior football in 1938; after RAF wartime service he made his league debut in 1946, winning a title medal that season and an FA Cup runners-up medal in 1950. His loyalty, versatility and consistency illuminated Anfield's gloomy era in the old Second Division. His deeds were such that the club was dubbed 'Liddellpool'; he and Sir Stanley Matthews were the only players to appear in the two Great Britain teams to take the field. An exemplary sportsman, he was never booked yet throughout his career he trained only twice a week due to his accountancy work. 'Billy would be beyond price in any era,' proclaimed his fellow legend Bob Paisley.

Then, during the installation of the new Main Stand at Anfield in 2016, Billy's bench in celebration of him being one of 'The Men Who Built Anfield' was erected, which also reads:

'A True Gentleman'

Liddell made his league debut for the club and scored twice in arguably the best game of what turned out to be a memorable title-winning season, the first of the post-war era.

While also reading 'LIDDELLPOOL' along one side.

These examples of the club honouring Billy show his importance, but the fact that he still has a flag that is flown on the Kop may have meant more. The fans at Liverpool have a great appreciation of honouring former players. At the empty stadium matches that came with the COVID-19 pandemic during the 2019/20 and 2020/21 seasons, Billy's flag sat proudly on the Kop throughout. Based to the right of the goal, it was seen on TV every week, particularly when Liverpool secured their first league title in 30 years. The story of the flag's inception is also interesting, as told by Rob Storry:

In 2006, Peter Etherington formed his website ontheKop.com, to bring his many match-going friends together, to form an online community and to extend this to other like-minded supporters. One of those great friends, Ian Graves, having visited Bob Paisley's hometown of Hetton-le-Hole, realised that there was a need for a memorial for Bob. After organising fundraising events and collections via the website, the memorial to Bob and the banner in the Kop were both unveiled in 2008.

Not long after the Paisley banner was unveiled, thoughts and discussions on the website turned to who should be honoured next. As the greatest and most successful manager became the centrepiece of the Kop banners, a decision on which player should be done needed to be made among the group.

Now when it comes to discussions on the greatest player of all time, there's generally one of three names at the top of every list, depending on your era. Steven Gerrard, Kenny Dalglish, and Billy Liddell. As Gerrard and Dalglish were well represented banner-wise, the choice of Billy Liddell became both an obvious and long overdue one.

Work set about with a design, and as with any player banners, a simple yet iconic image works best. When it comes to photographs, it's by no means an easy task to transfer images from camera to banner. This sort of technical expertise is where the website forum community often come together to help out, and our friend Steve – Macphisto80 from RAWK – was instrumental in bringing this part of the process together, and without whom we wouldn't have a banner with an image as brilliantly clear as it is.

The banner made its debut at Anfield on 24 October 2010, prior to the 2-1 win against Blackburn

Rovers, and was received almost as rapturously as Gerry Marsden, who appeared on the pitch singing 'You'll Never Walk Alone' that day.

Even now, so many years after making his last appearance for the club, there are still many supporters who absolutely worship Billy. The lads who also hold up the banner, Jay Graham, Ged Parkinson and Niall Cave, will all say that never a time goes by without someone stopping at the banner to talk about Billy, whether it be a memory of watching him play or of meeting him. Fellas will stop to stare at or touch the banner, lads who have his autograph because they lived close by or went to the same barbers as him will show us these treasured items held in their wallets.

The banner has even visited the memorial in Townhill, which friends from the OTK website visited on the weekend 'Three Memorials Tour', including those to both Bob Paisley and Bill Shankly.

The banner can be seen several times a season in the Kop, and also pictures we have taken can be seen on our Twitter account @OTKFLAGS

Having your legacy honoured by supporters 60 years after the last match you played for them is an incredible honour for Billy. It is not only Liverpool that has honoured him. In 2008, he was inducted into the Scottish Football Hall of Fame alongside Jim Leighton, Archie Gemmill, Derek Johnstone, Bobby Evans, Ian St John, John Thomson and Bill Struth. Then in 2016 he was inducted to the English National Football Museum where Ian Callaghan and Billy's grandsons accepted the honour on his behalf.

In 2010, after much media support, the Billy Liddell Memorial Group managed to have the memorial cairn in Townhill unveiled. This has been discussed at the start of the book, but again shows how all aspects of Billy's football life have made efforts to permanently honour his importance to them. There are yearly tournaments in his name in Townhill as well, ensuring the younger residents learn of his importance to their village.

Another way in which Liddell's legacy will be permanently remembered is through Liddell Avenue in Melling, a road named after him. Wheeler Drive, a couple of streets down, was also named after former team-mate Johnny Wheeler.

Billy's importance to Liverpool is further evidenced by the various votes that the club has arranged since his death. The 2002 vote for the '100 Days that Shook the Kop' had Billy's disallowed goal against Man City as the 40th most significant day. In 2006 and 2013, there was a vote for 'The 100 Players Who Shook the Kop', Liddell finishing sixth and eighth, respectively. In celebration of the 125th anniversary of Liverpool FC, the club unveiled its '50 Men Who Made LFC' and Billy came ninth.

It is nice to be able to present this book and not try to finish by pushing for his memory to be respected. It is inevitable that as time passes Billy will slip down lists as fewer people will be alive that recall seeing him running down the wing and unleashing a deadly shot on goal. Hopefully, by seeing his bench, plaque, flag, inductions, and maybe this book, Billy's name can live on. Any Liverpool, Scotland or football fan should learn the story of a man so important that he continues to be relevant 60 years after his retirement and 100 years since his birth.

This book would not exist without the help of Rena Liddell, who has been able to continue the Liddell and Liverpool connection, living so close to the ground and still attending every home match. The club has kept her involved as well, inviting her to attend the 125th anniversary dinner held at the stadium. From the poor way Billy was treated in the 1970s, it is good that the Liddell name is revered so highly today. It feels most appropriate that the final words written are from Rena:

> Billy Liddell played for Liverpool and received many an accolade. He was very happy in what he did, he wasn't a boaster and didn't go on about what he had done. He enjoyed playing and was so happy doing what he loved. He also enjoyed life after football, in the Guild, up until he retired, but most of all he was my brother and family through and through. I

had five brothers and they were no different to each other, he was just the most well-known. I think back and remember the time we spent together, which was lovely. I'm lucky that we had such a nice family.

Records and Statistics

William Beveridge Liddell, Records and Statistics
1938–1961

Liverpool Wartime

		Wartime – LFC	
		Matches	*Goals*
1939/40	...	16	9
1940/41	...	37	12
1941/42	...	36	22
1942/43	...	15	5
1943/44	...	6	4
1944/45	...	15	13
1945/46	...	29	18
Totals	...	154	83

Scotland

		International	
		Matches	*Goals*
1945/46	...	1	2
1946/47	...	2	0
1947/48	...	3	0
1948/49	...	–	–
1949/50	...	4	0

1950/51	...	4	2
1951/52	...	6	1
1952/53	...	3	1
1953/54	...	1	0
1954/55	...	4	2
1955/56	...	1	0
Totals	...	29	8

Liverpool

		Liverpool Matches	Goals
1945/46	...	2	1
1946/47	...	40	8
1947/48	...	39	11
1948/49	...	42	9
1949/50	...	48	19*
1950/51	...	36	15*
1951/52	...	43	19*
1952/53	...	40	13*
1953/54	...	37	7
1954/55	...	44	31*
1955/56	...	44	32*
1956/57	...	42	21*
1957/58	...	40	23
1958/59	...	19	14
1959/60	...	17	5
1960/61	...	1	0
Totals	...	534	228

*Liverpool's top goalscorer that season

1954/55 season Liddell was top league scorer (30), John Evans top in league and cup (33) with two more than Liddell.

Highlights of Billy Liddell's Football Career:

1930/31
Played for the first time for his school team, aged eight.

1935/36
Capped twice by Scotland in Schoolboy international matches.

1937/38
Played for Kingseat Juveniles and had trials with Blairhall Colliery, Hearts of Beath and Partick Thistle prior to being sought out by Liverpool and signed as an amateur in the close season.

1938/39
Signed his first professional forms for Liverpool on 17 April 1939, three months after his 17th birthday. The delay was caused by a bad knee injury received at Blackburn in an A team match.

1939/40
Played his first senior match for Liverpool against Crewe at Anfield on 1 January 1940.

1941/42
Joined the RAF, eventually attaining commissioned rank. Made his debut for Scotland in a wartime substitute match against England at Hampden Park, and scored a goal. Scotland won 5-4.

1942/43
Played for Scotland in two wartime matches against England, at Wembley in October and at Hampden Park in April. Broke his leg in a match for his RAF unit at

Bridgnorth (Shropshire). Posted to Canada for navigational training.

1945/46
Played four times this season for Scotland in wartime internationals, while still in the RAF.

1946/47
Demobilised and made his Football League debut against Chelsea at Anfield, scoring two goals, on 7 September 1946. Played for Great Britain against the Rest of Europe, and twice for Scotland. Liverpool won the First Division championship.

1947/48
Chosen three times for Scotland.

1948/49
Played in one match for Liverpool at centre-forward this season, occupying four forward positions during the campaign.

1949/50
Got a losing FA Cup medal with Liverpool to add to his championship medal. Liverpool were unbeaten until the 20th match of the season. Leading scorer for the club. Chosen another four times for Scotland.

1950/51
Won another four caps with Scotland, but missed the summer tour, as Liverpool took him with them to Sweden. Top scorer again.

1951/52
Played six times for Scotland this season, and again leading Liverpool marksman.

1952/53

Another three caps. Played eight matches for Liverpool at centre-forward. Top scorer again.

1953/54

Played only once for Scotland. Again occupied four different forward positions for Liverpool.

1954/55

Took over the leadership of the Liverpool forward line permanently in the seventh match of the season. Finished up with 30 league goals and top marksman for the fifth time. Another four Scottish caps added to his collection.

1955/56

Appointed captain of the Liverpool team for the first of three seasons. Top scorer once more with 27 league goals. Chosen for the Great Britain team against the Rest of Europe at Belfast, being the only other player besides Stanley Matthews to play in both Great Britain matches. Capped by Scotland for the last time on 8 October 1955.

1956/57

Leading Liverpool marksman again, with 21 league goals.

1957/58

Beat Elisha Scott's record of 429 league appearances, then the highest total by any Liverpool player, when appearing against Notts County at Anfield on 9 November 1957. Top Liverpool league scorer for the eighth time in nine years with 22 league goals.

1958/59

Handed over the captaincy to Johnny Wheeler, but still giving the club fine service. Scored 14 in 19 league matches. When omitted from the cup tie against Worcester

City it was the first Liddell had missed for the club in post-war football. Played his 466th league match against Barnsley on 27 March 1958, thus beating the previous best total by any senior Merseyside club player, that of 465 by Ted Sagar for Everton. Completed 200 league goals in the first week of the season.

1959/60
Limited to 17 first-team matches, the lowest of his career, but still giving useful assistance when called upon.

1960/61
Played his 534th and final match for Liverpool in a 1-0 loss to Southampton at Anfield in August 1960. Awarded a testimonial in honour of his 23-year Anfield career.

References

Books:

Barclay, Patrick, *Sir Matt Busby: The Man Who Made a Football Club*

Barnes, Walley, *Captain of Wales*

Barrett, Norman, *The Daily Telegraph Football Chronicle*

Burgess, Ron, *Football: My Life*

Finney, Tom, *Tom Finney: My Autobiography,*

Greaves, Jimmy, *The Heart of the Game*

Herbert, Ian, *Quiet Genius: Bob Paisley, British Football's Greatest Manager*

Hill, Jimmy, *Great Soccer Stars*

Keith, John, *Billy Liddell: The Legend Who Carried the Kop*

Lamming, Doug, *Who's Who of Liverpool: 1892-1989,*

Liddell, Billy, *My Soccer Story*

Matthews, Tony, *Who's Who of Liverpool,*

Mortensen, Stanley, *Football is My Game*

Paul, Roy, *A Red Dragon of Wales: The Autobiography of Roy Paul*

Pawson, Tony, *The Goalscorers: From Bloomer to Keegan*

Sharpe, Ivan, *Soccer Top Ten*

REFERENCES

Shaw, Gary and Platt, Mark, *At the End of the Storm*

Taylor, Rogan and Ward, Andrew, *Three Sides of the Mersey: An Oral History of Everton, Liverpool and Tranmere Rovers*

Walmsley, David, *Liverpool's Greatest Players: The Official Guide*

Wright, Billy, *The World's My Football Pitch*

Young, George, *Captain of Scotland*

Interviews:

Adrian Killen

Alan Banks

Alan Hansen

Alex South

Betty Liddell

Bill Hughes

Billy Howard

Billy Shine

David Liddell

Dominic Myers

Doug Cowie

Frank Cann

Fred Wilson

George Scott

Gordon Milne

Gordon Wallace

Greg Symon

Ian Callaghan

Ian Tracey

Jamie Carragher

Jimmy Melia

John Carey

John Kennedy

Johnny Morrissey

Keith Burkinshaw

Malcolm Liddell

Norman Gard

Pat Martin

Paul McNulty

Paul Moran

Rena Liddell

Rob Storry

Ron Schofield

Stephen Shaw

Tom Ogilvie

Websites:

BritishNewspaperArchive.co.uk

LFChistory.net Arnie Baldursson and Gudmundur Magnusson

PlayUpLiverpool.com Kjell Hanssen

Index

Spence, Dick 73
Spicer, Eddie 91, 96, 137, 144
St John, Ian 73, 115, 161, 224, 241, 269
Steel, Billy 198, 206, 208–209
Steffen, Willi 210
Stein, Jock 242
Stewart, George 101
Struth, Bill 269
Stubbins, Albert 93–96, 99–100, 103, 112, 116, 122–124, 159, 242
Suárez, Luis 63, 157
Swift, Frank 209
Swindin, George 123

T
Tanner, Bill 73–74
Tarbuck, Jimmy 235
Taylor, Phil 61, 84, 94, 96, 110, 121, 181, 183–184, 192, 215, 230–231
Telfer, Willie 203
Telford, George 72, 87
Thomas, Clive 185–186
Thomas, Dick 162
Thompson, Phil 242
Thomson, John 269
Tracey, Bill 71
Trautmann, Bert 186
Travassos, José 211
Turnbull, Eddie 200
Twentyman, Geoff 235

V
van Brandt, Alfons 210
Vaughan, Frankie 142
Vernon, Jackie 209
Vincent, Jean 211
Vukas, Bernard 211

W
Waddell, Willie 198
Wainwright, Eddie 118

Also available at all good book stores

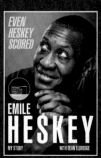

9781785315008

9781909626584

9781785314407

9781785313967

9781785310423

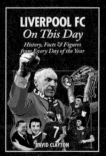

9781908051059

9781908051677

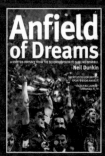

9781905449804

9781785311932